How

not

to

stay

Single

10 *steps*

to a great

relationship

Nita Tucker

with Randi Moret

Crown Trade Paperbacks
New York

Published by Crown Publishers, Inc., 201 East 50th Street,
New York, New York 10022.
Member of the Crown Publishing Group.

Random House, Inc. New York, Toronto, London, Sydney,
Auckland
http://www.randomhouse.com/

CROWN TRADE PAPERBACKS and colophon are trademarks of
Crown Publishers, Inc.

Printed in the United States of America

Design by Linda Kocur

Library of Congress Cataloging-in-Publication Data
CIP TK

ISBN 0-517-88637-5 (pbk.)

10 9 8 7 6 5 4 3 2 1

First Edition

This book is dedicated to Tony, my husband and the love of my life.

acknowledgments

Special thanks to

my agent, Maureen Walters, for not giving up on me.

Shaye Areheart and Frac Fox for their contributions to this book.

my coauthor, Randi Moret, for making this book great.

Kim Dower and Terry and Alan Axelrod for always being there for me.

Gabe and Larry Burke for making my life so fun.

my children, Jordan and Montana, for making me a mom—the best thing that has ever happened to me.

contents

introduction

a lot of us have had relationships that made our lives worse. Most single people would rather be alone than in a bad relationship. This book is about having a relationship that supports and enhances your life and makes it better.

 *

I used to travel a lot when I was single and working as a management consultant. When I would return to my hotel room after an intense day spent with high-powered clients, my first impulse was always to call home—to tell them about my exciting day and let them know where I was. I'd reach for the phone, then realize there was no one who needed to know how to get in touch with me or who was waiting to hear about my day.

It was always when I felt fulfilled and excited that I would reach for the phone to call home. For most of us, it's when life is great that we want a relationship. We want someone to share the good times with. When we're depressed and feeling miserable, a bag of cookies will do just fine.

It's not that I think everyone should be in a relationship or that everyone should want one. Relationships aren't for everyone. One of the great things about the times we live in is that there are so many lifestyle choices available. If you want to stay single, I think that's great—and this book isn't for you (although I can't stop your relatives from buying it for you).

Most books about relationships fall into two categories: They either tell you how to trap, manipulate, trick, or seduce someone into a relationship, or they tell you the reason you don't have one is because there's something wrong with you that you have to fix. Many singles have been brainwashed into believing they're single because they're psychologically impaired. However, if you're like most singles, there's something wrong with what you're doing, not with who you are. This book is about changing what you're doing. It's not about changing you.

I wrote this book because, when I was single, I needed a book like this. I had always imagined myself married with children and a station wagon by the age of thirty. When my mother was that age, she was going on her third child. But when I turned thirty, I was going on my fifth year without a date. I decided I wanted a relationship—not because I was supposed to have one, but because I wanted to share my life with someone. I listened to my friends, who told me that when you're not looking, that's when you'll find someone (I dispel this popular myth in the step 2 chapter). I followed their advice. Two years and no dates later, I decided to take action. I took the steps that are outlined in this book, inventing them as I went along. The result was that I found the man of my dreams—and we've been happily married for the last fourteen years.

I didn't realize it at the time, but in retrospect I can see that not only was I taking steps to find a relationship for myself, I was also developing a "curriculum" for others to follow. When my friends saw that I had the kind of relationship I always wanted, they started asking me for advice. I told them the steps I had taken. A lot of them took the same actions and found relationships, too.

More people started calling. Discovering there was a widespread need for this information, I developed a course, drawing on my experiences as a teacher, seminar leader, and consultant. I began giving "Connecting: How to Find a Lifetime Relationship" seminars in Seattle, Washington, in 1985. That evolved into the "How Not to Stay Single" course, which I have been doing since 1991 in thirty cities throughout the United States and Canada. This book is based on my seminars and the experiences of the thousands of single people who have attended them.

Being single can be fun, and it can also be funny. In television programs such as "Seinfeld" and comic strips such as "Cathy" that make fun of single lifestyles, singles can find humor in their situation and laugh at themselves. This is a good thing. But when you're alone and you don't want to be, it's not a joke.

If you follow the steps on these pages, you *will* find a relationship—just like the majority of people who have taken my seminars. Many of them thought they could never find a relationship because they were too old, too fat, or too poor, or because they had kids or traveled too much. You may think there is some reason you can't find a relationship. But you can; just as they discovered they could.

This book is a workbook. At the end of each chapter there is a list of "assignments," things to do to enable you to reach your goal of having a great relationship. These activities are not optional. Just as reading a book about dieting without altering your eating habits would not result in weight loss, simply reading this book won't change your life. The assignments are what enable you to put the principles of this book into practice, which is the only way your success can be guaranteed. Following the steps outlined in this book will not always be easy, but it *will* lead you to a relationship—the kind of relationship you have always wanted.

How
not
to
stay
Single

come out of the closet

✻

i usually begin my "How Not to Stay Single" seminars with the question: How many people here are single? Not surprisingly, just about everyone raises their hands. I then ask them to raise their hands if they want to find a relationship. Only about five out of a hundred people do.

If I asked the people in the "Finding a Job On-line" class down the hall whether they hoped to get a job through the Internet, I think most if not all of them would say yes. I don't think people in the "Investing in Real Estate" seminar would be shy about admitting they were interested in buying property, and I doubt if the "How to Become a Travel Writer" students would deny they hope to get paid for traveling. So there's something a little suspect about the fact that the people in the "How Not to Stay Single" seminars all refuse to admit they want relationships.

Think about it. If you were sitting in my seminar, would you raise your hand? Probably not. You'd probably be afraid that everyone would stare at you, that you would be the only person in your row to admit you are looking.

My seminar isn't the only place where singles are hiding in the closet. Walk into a singles' bar sometime and ask people what they're doing there. I've done it. People told me they were there to kill an hour, to unwind, or they were just stopping by for a drink on their way home from work. Anything but admitting that they were there to meet prospective mates.

Whenever I think about this, I'm reminded of my friend Ed, an author of military novels. I gave him a copy of my previous book about this subject, which he read on an airplane. He told me later he had placed the book inside the dust jacket of *History of the Marines, World War II* so that no one would see what he was reading.

Think back to when you bought this book. Were you embarrassed while you stood in line at the cashier? Do you cover up the title when you read it in a public place?

if you're so great, *why are you still* single?

The reason so many single people deny that they want a relationship is because they're ashamed of wanting one. They are also ashamed of not having one. This shame is a reaction to the stigma that was attached to being single when most of us were growing up. Thirty years ago, the word "single" wasn't even used to describe someone who wasn't married. You were an "un." If you were over twenty-five and unmarried, there was something wrong with you. It was a shame on your whole family.

The words "spinster" and "old maid" can still make most single women cringe. Being a bachelor was more acceptable, but men were not exempt from the stigma. As a kid, there was an unmarried man who lived down the street from us. I remember getting a clear impression from the grownups around me that he was weird. On Halloween, we knew we weren't supposed to go to his house.

Thankfully, today no one thinks there's something wrong with you because you're not married—except of course your mother. It has become socially acceptable to be single.

That's good, but there's a backlash: Now that it is all right to be alone, we're stigmatizing wanting a relationship.

People are afraid that wanting a relationship means they're needy, desperate, and codependent. They're afraid people will say, "Oh, you want a relationship. That means you're not 'whole.' You think you need someone else to love you because you don't love yourself."

People are buying into the idea that if they want a relationship there must be something lacking in themselves. This is a tragedy.

I find that women are worse than men in this regard. A single woman I met recently at a party is a typical example. I asked her if she was interested in finding a relationship (I'm an incorrigible matchmaker), and she answered that her job was really fulfilling. This is like asking someone if they want a new car and having them say, "No, I already have a set of good china."

nothing *to be ashamed of*

If you really think about it, this shame is idiotic. Wanting someone with whom to share your life isn't like wanting to molest children or embezzle money. There is nothing to be ashamed of here.

Having a life partner is a natural and basic human impulse and can be one of life's greatest enrichments. If it's a good idea to have a relationship, why would it be bad to want one?

Wanting to love someone and be loved does not mean there's something wrong with you. In fact, wanting a relationship is more a sign that you are healthy, normal, and well-functioning than that you are lacking in some way.

Being ashamed of wanting a relationship may be absurd, but it is the number one factor sabotaging people's hopes and dreams of finding a life partner.

My advice is to throw off this misplaced sense of shame. If you must feel ashamed, find something less self-defeating to be embarrassed about. How about the fact that you are wearing the same pair of socks you wore yesterday, or that you haven't watered your plants all week?

The first step to finding a relationship is to admit to yourself that you want one. Yes, I know that not everyone wants a relationship, that some people actually prefer being single. I'm not talking to those people. I'm talking to you. You're the one reading this book.

If you let embarrassment keep you from admitting you want a relationship, you will be much less effective at finding one. If you wanted a job, you would put the word out to friends and associates, scour the want ads, maybe call a headhunter. You wouldn't be embarrassed that you wanted a job, so you would take the steps and use the resources that could lead you to one. That's what you need to do in the area of relationships.

Start telling people you're looking for a relationship. Telling people what you want and asking for their support is one of the most effective ways of getting what you want. You may still feel a sense of embarrassment at first, but tell them anyway. Taking action is the most effective way to dispel those feelings. If you keep *acting* as if you're not embarrassed, pretty soon you won't feel embarrassed. Try to catch yourself when you start waffling on this or getting defensive.

By the way, nothing makes you sound more needy than trying to cover up that you want something. When you say, "My life is fine; I don't need anyone," you sound defensive. When you are direct and upfront about what you want, you appear confident and self-assured.

After some practice, you should be able to say, "I'm looking for a relationship, do you know anybody you could fix me up with?" as easily as you could say, "I'm looking for a good gardener, do you know anyone you could recommend?"

People who take my seminars always arrive on the first night expecting to be surrounded by a bunch of losers. They are always surprised to find the other participants are attractive, successful, happy people. It makes it easier for them to realize that wanting a relationship is nothing to be ashamed of.

step 1 assignments

1. List all the reasons you have used to justify why you don't have a relationship: for example, I'm too discriminating; there aren't enough single men/women in this city; no one wants someone with kids. It should become evident that many of these excuses just cover up your fear that being single means there is something wrong with you.

2. List all the reasons why you are ashamed or embarrassed about the fact that you don't have a relationship:

for example, it means I'm unlovable; it means I'm too needy.

3. List all the reasons why you are ashamed or embarrassed about the fact that you want a relationship: for example, it means I'm desperate; it means I can't make it on my own.

Take a minute to honestly evaluate whether the concerns you listed in exercises 2 and 3 are legitimate or just bogus ideas you have unwittingly accepted.

4. Write an essay entitled, "Why I Want a Relationship."

5. Tell five friends you're looking for a relationship.

stop wishing and hoping

*

"When you're not looking, that's when you'll find a relationship." If you're like most people, you believe this statement wholeheartedly. But that doesn't make it true. What is true is that this false belief is preventing you from finding a relationship.

Successful salespeople don't talk about their prospects showing up "when the timing is right." You don't hear bankers or stockbrokers saying they find the best investment opportunities when they're "not looking." Executives don't let the success of their companies "just happen." Yet many of these same people believe a relationship will come along when they're not focusing on it. It's why so many people who are successful in their careers are unsuccessful in their love lives.

One reason people believe that a relationship is something that just happens, rather than something they have to make happen, is because that's the romantic ideal with which most of us were raised. Our images of how romantic love should come about are derived from cultural archetypes. It may have worked for Sleeping Beauty or Rapunzel, but most women are not going to meet their prince while they're at home sleeping or washing their hair. Most men are not going to encounter a beautiful damsel in distress while commuting to and from the office.

We understand that making something happen in our careers requires planning, perseverence, time, and hard work, but we think finding a relationship shouldn't. We're enamored with the idea of fate intervening and putting us in just the right place at just the right time to meet our true love. We think that if it's "meant to be," we'll meet someone while we're walking the dog or by answering a wrong number.

This does happen, you may argue. Your cousin Irving was at home one night when someone came to the door canvassing for a political candidate and they both immediately knew this was "it." Yes, we all know one or two people who found a relationship when they weren't looking. They are the exceptions, but we use their stories to keep the myth going. You may not like it, but the fact is that statistically, staying at home and doing nothing is not a very good way to meet people.

My friend Rebecca is a die-hard romantic. "I would never want to meet someone through a personal ad or at a singles' bar, because it's just not romantic," she says. "Love should be magical, not something you engineer." Rebecca, an attractive women who lives in a large city, is going on her third year without a date. While she's waiting for Fate to send someone to her, she's spending her nights in the most unromantic way possible—alone.

I'm all for romance, and I'd love it if everyone could meet their true love through a cosmic twist of fate. But is how you meet someone really so important? Isn't it more important that your relationship be romantic and magical *after* you get together? Wouldn't you like to increase the chances that you will meet someone with whom you can experience lasting romance? Waiting and wishing will not help you do that.

the reality *behind the* myth

Until recently, most people met their mates at school, when they were in their late teens and early twenties. These are the people who helped create the myth, "When you least expect it, that's when you'll find someone."

Doing nothing worked for you when you were in school. You met people all the time, without looking and without trying. It doesn't seem right that now you have to make a special effort.

But if you think about it, you weren't really "doing nothing" to meet people in school. You were constantly participating in activities—attending classes; going to dances, parties, and club functions—that brought you into contact with members of the opposite sex. Every meeting, extracurricular activity, sports event, or snack was a social opportunity. You were always making new friends, both male and female, and then meeting their friends and their friends' friends.

The "spontaneous" relationships you had in school were actually the result of a tremendous amount of socializing. You just didn't notice you were socializing because it was what everyone was doing, all the time.

School was the ideal environment for connecting with the opposite sex: Most people were in the same age group and single. To meet them, all you had to do was show up. Even studying was an opportunity to socialize. (Why do you think you studied in the library? Because it was quiet?)

You met new people from morning until night and, lo and behold, when you least expected it, when you were focused on something else, a relationship magically materialized.

Another factor that made relationships happen more easily when you were in school is that you didn't put the same significance on them that you do now. You were more open. You didn't say, "I can't date someone in my English Lit class; it might not work out and then we'd still have to go to class together for the whole semester." Going out for a Coke was going out for a Coke—not your only hope of avoiding being alone for the rest of your life. No wonder relationships "just happened."

that was then, *this is* now

Now that people are waiting until they're older to mate, the social situations they once took for granted are no longer a primary part of their lives. You go to work and come home, and wonder why relationships don't spontaneously materialize the way they used to. Unless you live at Melrose Place, the probability of meeting someone when you're at home is pretty slim. And it's doubtful that you're going to get a message on your voice mail at work, when you least expect it, saying, "Hello, I'm the one you've been waiting for. My beeper number is ——."

The hard, cold truth is that if you want to meet members of the opposite sex, you're going to have to make a special effort to put yourself in situations where you're likely to come in contact with them. I changed my strategy from waiting, wishing, and hoping to taking purposeful action, and four months later I found a relationship.

Here's how it happened: I was in Bali, one of the most romantic countries in the world. I had met a man who was tall, good-looking, sensitive, fun—and a doctor! I recognized him immediately: He was the man I had been dreaming of.

We were walking along a ridge overlooking a beautiful vista. The sunset was magnificent. He looked into my eyes; I looked up into his, ready for our first kiss. He said three magic words, words that were to change the direction of my life. They were: "Nita, I'm gay." (I'm not kidding; this really happened!)

I saw my future flash before me. An ancient Chinese proverb says, "If we do not change our direction, we are likely to end up where we are headed." I saw that all my fantasizing and hoping had gotten me nowhere, and that unless I did something else, I was likely to end up alone.

Right then and there I made a commitment. I resolved to find a relationship. I didn't know what it would take, but I was going to find out, and I was going to do it.

When I returned home, I did some research and discovered that Seattle, Washington, was a good place to meet single men. I had a successful career, terrific friends, and a nice home in San Francisco, but finding a relationship was more important to me than holding on to my comfortable lifestyle. I got all my belongings together, sold my house, and moved to Seattle. (It was the heyday of women's lib and I admit that I lied about why I was making this move to avoid being scorned by everyone I knew.)

In Seattle, I began applying the same kind of energy and perseverance that had made me successful in business to my new project, that of finding a relationship. I did everything I could think of. I told everyone I met that I was looking for a relationship and asked if they knew anyone they could fix me up with. I went to every party I could find and to art galleries, restaurants, bars, and other places where I thought the kind of men I wanted to meet would go. I went out three or four nights a week.

Was it fun? Of course not. The only people who think dating is fun are married people who haven't done it in years.

Was it worth it? Absolutely. I met a man with whom I fell madly in love. We've been happily married for the last fourteen years.

I'm not saying you have to move to a new city and do everything I did in order to find a relationship. What I am saying is that you have to make a commitment to reaching your goal and to taking whatever action is necessary to reach it. In other words, you have to make this a project.

project relationship

There's a difference between "making something a project" and "hoping it will turn out." The difference is in your level of commitment and your responsibility for reaching your goal.

When you undertake a project, you assume there will be a tangible end result and that you will reach it. When you set out to buy a house, you expect to end up with a house. When you enroll in school to become a real estate agent, you expect to get your license. When you decide to open a branch office, you know one will open. The question about a project isn't whether something will happen at the end, but how and when it will happen.

You understand that this approach is effective in other fields of endeavor, but you think finding a relationship is different. It's not. You need to adopt the same attitude toward finding a relationship that you would toward any other important undertaking.

I can hear you whining: "That's so manipulative. How can something spontaneous happen when it's all part of a plan?" I have traveled all over the world and not once did a pair of tickets to India show up in my mailbox when I least expected it. It took making it a project—planning the dates, saving the money, deciding where I would go. I'm sure there are plenty of examples in your own life where you took the time to arrange to have something important happen. You didn't consider that manipulative. Why have a double standard when it comes to relationships?

Another complaint I hear a lot is, "I'm not comfortable with the dating scene—it's not me." I hate to break it to you, but this process is not about you being comfortable. Comfort is being home, alone, under an afghan, watching TV in a robe with no waistband, eating. Just about everything else is uncomfortable. So if you're waiting for this whole dating thing to be comfortable, you may have to wait a very long time. You're going to have to make getting what you want in life more important than being comfortable.

My success came when I stopped thinking of a relationship as something that was in the hands of fate and began thinking of it as a project that was under my control. I applied the same skills that had made me successful in other areas of my life to finding a relationship. The same thing will work for you.

If you're not convinced, ask yourself how long you have been waiting for the right person to cross your path. How much longer are you willing to wait? This will probably be the most important relationship of your life. Do you really want to leave it to chance?

step 2 assignments

1. Choose a support person/partner.

The first thing to do once you make a commitment to finding a relationship is to enlist the aid of a "partner" or "support person," someone who is also committed to seeing you reach your goal. It can be a man or a woman, a single friend, a married friend, or a relative. The ideal partner is another person who is also looking for a relationship.

Being able to talk to this person when you feel discouraged and knowing that she or he is there to support you will make your project a lot easier and help ensure its success. Now you can say, "I went to a party and talked to five men/women," and not have to hear, "How could you do that? I'd never do that." Instead, a good support partner might say, "How did you do that? I want to be able to do that, too."

Your support person must be someone who is willing to get tough with you if that's what's needed. If you say, "I'm too busy to go out," she or he should say, "I don't want to hear any excuses—do you want a relationship or not?"

2. Make a promise to your support person about a specific action you will take this week that will help you move toward finding a relationship.

3. Write an essay about your "ideal relationship."

List the qualities that are important to you: how you are together, what you do together, how you communicate. Don't describe what you want in terms of what you don't want. For example, instead of, "He doesn't place a lot of demands on my time," say, "He is respectful of my life and my commitments." Instead of, "She doesn't try to change me," say, "She makes me feel appreciated and adored."

Share the essay with your partner.

set yourself free

*

When I tell people it's important to be available in order to find a relationship, they usually couldn't agree more. They're angry that so many people who are unavailable are out there dating, pretending to be available. They're afraid of becoming the unsuspecting victim of such a detestable person. They want advice on how to recognize and identify people who are unavailable so they can steer clear of them.

Then I ask them whether they are available. Sometimes they get a little defensive: "Of course I'm available. I'm looking for a relationship"; "I'm open to finding the right person. I'm taking this seminar, aren't I?"

Let's find out what you think. The following stories are from people who have taken my seminars. Which of these four people do you consider to be available?

number 1: "I'm waiting for the right person to show up, but I'm not going to waste my time with someone who doesn't have what I'm looking for. She has to have a great body, be athletic, financially independent, not smoke, want and be able to have children, not mind if I play golf three times a week or go out drinking with my friends, and not need a lot of attention. Find me someone like that and I'll jump at the chance to get involved with her."

* *number 2:* "I know she doesn't love me now. But we have a good time and she shows signs that she cares. She wouldn't keep going out with me if she didn't really like me. In fact, I think she's just afraid to admit how much she cares. If I keep hanging in there and make it safe for her, I know she'll come around. In the meantime, I'm dating other women and if I meet one that compares to her, I'll end it."

* *number 3:* "I was in denial but now I realize he's never going to leave his wife. I love him and I know he loves me, too, but there's no future in it. That's why I want to meet someone else. I'm open to dating, but until someone great comes along, at least there is someone who fulfills my needs."

* *number 4:* "I'm hoping Mr. Right will come along. In the meantime, being single can be lonely, and I'm seeing this other guy. He's nice and sweet and really likes me. I know he would like it to be more and sometimes I worry about leading him on, but I've told him the truth: There's no future in this relationship. I think of him as a friend I can have sex with. When I get lonely or need an escort, he's there for me."

These four people have one thing in common—with each other and with a majority of other single people: They think they are available, but, really, they aren't. They took my seminar in the hope that it would help them find mates. It was a rude awakening for them to realize that it was their own unavailability that prevented them from finding the kind of relationships they wanted.

These four stories typify the situations I hear about most often from people in my seminars. Let's analyze what makes these people unavailable.

Number 1 is looking for the perfect woman, but he'll never find her. It's not too hard to imagine that even if he miraculously met someone who lived up to his impossible criteria, she would still somehow fall short of his ideal of perfection. In Chapter 6 we'll go more deeply into the question of how to effectively screen people. But you should know that if you're unwilling to go out and meet new people or to spend time with anyone who isn't "perfect," you are not available.

The remaining three stories are about people who are unavailable because they are already in relationships. Being in a dead-end, or "go-nowhere," relationship is by far the most prevalent circumstance preventing people from finding someone with whom they could have a real relationship, which is why we're going to explore this phenomenon in detail.

When you are in a dead-end relationship, you are not available. It's kind of like: If the seat next to you on the bus is taken, no one is going to sit down in it. I can't tell you how many people I've known who insisted they were "open" despite being in a go-nowhere relationship. They didn't meet anyone new, however, until they broke up with their dead-end lovers.

There are several kinds of go-nowhere relationships. Many people, like numbers 2 and 3, are involved with people who are unavailable.

If you are involved with someone who is unavailable, stop hoping his or her situation will change, and move on. By staying with this person, you're virtually guaranteeing you will not find someone with whom you could have a truly satisfying relationship.

If you're going out with someone who is married, you're doubly sabotaging yourself, because being in this relationship contributes to you not feeling good about yourself. People often justify going out with someone who's married by saying things like, "Her marriage was already over," or "He's just staying with her because of the kids." Even if you're not the cause of the marriage breaking up, being with a married person corrodes your sense of self-worth. And self-esteem is a prerequisite for a good relationship.

Number 4 is a woman who was involved in a close, sexual relationship with a guy to whom she had no intention of committing. This can be the most difficult kind of relationship to give up.

No one has ever fought me on this harder than Cynthia, a thirty-five-year-old management consultant who took my seminar several years ago. Convincing her to stop seeing Randy, a guy with whom she had been having a go-nowhere relationship for the previous three years, was like trying to pry a life preserver away from someone who was drowning.

Cynthia was quite a bit older than Randy, and she knew she would never want to marry him, but she hated the dating scene and didn't want to face the possibility of being rejected. Randy adored her and he was always there for her. It wasn't easy, but I finally convinced her to break up with him.

As she was soon to find out, breaking up wasn't enough. Shortly after they stopped seeing each other, Randy ran into some problems in his application to graduate school. He called her for help. She wanted to be his friend, so she agreed to get together with him.

You can probably guess what happened. It was late, it was so nice seeing each other again, blah blah blah. Anyway, they got back together.

Three months later, she broke it off again. Again, he had an emergency. Again, he called her. Again, she wanted to be a friend. Again, seeing each other brought them back together.

The same cycle occurred one more time before I was finally able to convince Cynthia that she had to stop being Randy's "friend." She saw that to be truly supportive, she would have to get out of his life; that by being there to bail him out of emergencies, she was making it impossible for either of them to move on.

She had broken up with him before; this time she gave him up. The loss was very painful, but eventually things worked out for everyone involved. Cynthia found a guy she was crazy about and married him. Randy, when he realized Cynthia really wasn't coming back, stopped hoping she would and stopped having emergencies. He found a woman who is crazy about him. Now that they each have mates, Randy and Cynthia still stay in touch. They have a genuine friendship.

Your dead-end lover will probably want to "stay friends" when you tell him or her that you want to break up. Be a true friend, and explain why this has to be done cold turkey. Explain that you'll be able to resume the friendship after you've both found other mates. Realize that merely saying the words is not going to get your point across. You're going to have to withdraw from the relationship, no matter how painful that may be for you or the other person. You're doing your "friend" a disservice by leading him or her on.

People give me all kinds of reasons why they shouldn't have to break up with their dead-end lovers:

"We're really just friends."

"She knows I go out with other women and it's okay."

"I've been seeing him for five years, and I've had several other relationships in between."

"At my age this is as good as it gets."

The real reason you cling to dead-end relationships is because you're afraid that nothing better will come along and you'll be alone. You want to wait until you find a replacement before you let go because you're afraid there will be a void in your life. You should understand that a genuine relationship is most likely to occur when there is just such a void.

If you are afraid of being alone, that is all the more reason to give up your dead-end relationship. If you want to have a great relationship, it's important that you find out you can live successfully without one.

Yes, you will be taking a risk if you give up your dead-end lover. There is no guarantee you will find someone to replace him or her. But think about what you're giving up by staying with that person. Think about the relationship you envisioned when you wrote your essay in exercise 3 in the last chapter. That's what you really want, and that's what you will probably never have if you don't take this risk.

Your project of finding a lifetime mate is going to require you to take a lot of risks, so you may as well start getting in the habit now.

Once you are sure of your own availability, it's time to focus on the people you date. How can you ensure that you won't get involved with someone who is unavailable?

With most people, it's pretty straightforward. Someone who is married is not available. A person who is living with someone or already in a long-term relationship is not available.

People who are separated or recently divorced are not quite as unavailable as those who are married. But they are often still focused on their ex, and may be embroiled in legal and financial matters as well. It isn't a hard-and-fast rule, but you should know that the median remarriage time for someone who has been divorced is forty-four months. A better rule of thumb than elapsed time is the amount of time a person spends talking about her or his ex.

If you are dating someone who is still getting over a former lover, don't allow yourself to be drawn into the process by engaging in extended conversations, dispensing advice, or being a shoulder for her or him to cry on. Instead, simply say that you don't feel comfortable talking about this. Otherwise, you risk becoming associated with the old relationship, and when your lover finally does get over it, she or he will have to leave *you*, too, in order to move on.

What if someone's words about their availability contradict their actions? In this case, it's usually best to believe their actions. An excellent guideline to help you determine whether someone is available is how much time they are spending with you. Basically, someone who cannot or does not make time to be with you is not available—despite their protestations to the contrary.

The opposite can also be true, as my friend Sharon discovered. She was dating a man who kept telling her he didn't want to get involved: he was married to his career; he wasn't interested in a relationship; he wasn't ready for a commitment; she shouldn't get her hopes up. Despite this running dialogue, he called her nearly every day, they saw each other almost every night, and he asked her to go on a vacation with him.

Sharon, believing what he said about his unavailability,

almost broke up with him. I told her I'd never seen anyone who was more available and that she should pay attention to his actions, not his words. She hung in there, and eventually they got married.

When my friend Sue moved in with her boyfriend, he warned her that he definitely had no intention of ever getting married. Her response was, "I don't remember asking you." She never brought it up again, but he did—when he proposed a year later.

A lot of people who really do want to get involved in permanent relationships think and say that they don't be- cause they're afraid. That they have fears about getting more deeply involved doesn't necessarily mean they are unavail- able. After all, many of the men and women who are now married and thrilled about it were once just as apprehensive.

If someone says they don't want a relationship but their actions tell you they do, don't give up on them too soon. Obviously, there will be a time when giving up on such a person becomes appropriate, but a lot of people make the mistake of doing this prematurely. (We'll talk about this more in the step 10 chapter.)

step 3 assignment

If you are in a dead-end relationship, break it off. If you think you'll be in danger of caving in, use your support person.

step **4**

be a great catch

> attract (e-trăkt), verb:
>
> 1. *To cause to draw near or adhere*
> 2. *To arouse or compel the interest,
>   admiration, or attention of.*
>
> —THE AMERICAN HERITAGE DICTIONARY OF
> THE ENGLISH LANGUAGE, 3rd ed.

are you waiting to find a relationship before you travel, take up skiing, or buy a house? Do you feel that your life can't be rich or satisfying until you've found your "other half?" Rather than putting your life on hold, you should be living it to the fullest right now. People are attractive when they are enjoying themselves and having a good time. The happier you are with your life, the more likely it is that someone will want to become a part of it. When you're turned on about yourself, other people are turned on to you.

This was really brought home to me when I was in Los Angeles with my friend Sarah. Sarah is a large woman, and although she is very pretty, you wouldn't consider her a knockout—especially in a city known for its worship of anorexic-looking bodies. When we started our trip, had you asked me which of us was better looking I would have said (modestly) that I was. I was certainly thinner than she. But by the end of three days I felt like chopped liver.

Men would literally stop Sarah on the street. They fawned all over her in restaurants and stores, barely noticing me. I realized they were attracted to the same thing I love about her. She is a happy, sparkling person who exudes joie de vivre. She is fun to be with. And she's not uptight about her size. She carries herself with confidence, obviously comfortable with herself just the way she is. And men trip over themselves to be around her.

It is often said that until you love yourself you can't love anyone else. I believe that unless you love yourself, you won't let anyone else love you. Having high self-esteem is essential not only to attacting people, but to maintaining a great relationship once you do find someone. A lack of confidence in yourself can be contagious, as I discovered one night shortly after Tony and I began living together.

Tony had come home from a "night out with the guys." He told me about a woman who had flirted with him at the bar where he and his friends had spent the evening.

He was not talking about this woman to make me jealous; he was just telling me about his night. It was clear that he had no interest in her. Nevertheless, hearing about this woman made me start to feel insecure about myself.

"Was she really pretty?" I asked him. "She was thinner than I am, wasn't she? I'll bet your friends thought you were a fool not to get her number."

As I expressed these insecurities, I noticed Tony's attitude subtly start to change. My doubts about myself seemed to be rubbing off on him. It was as though my lack of self-confidence undermined *his* confidence about his choice of me as his mate.

I guess my confidence in myself and my certainty that I was the right woman for Tony were stronger than my insecurities, because suddenly something clicked, and I saw there was nothing to be worried about. After all, I was the one he had come home to.

I said in a carefree way, "Well, of course, she might have a better body than me, but no one is better for you than me." He brightened. Whereas my doubts about myself had made him start to feel unsure, my confidence in myself made him feel good about being with me.

When I ask the people in my seminars if they think they're a "good catch," most of them have trouble answering affirmatively. When I ask them to list ten qualities that make them a good catch, many of them can't come up with a complete list.

Knowing that it's important to value and love yourself doesn't automatically make you do so. How, then, do you raise your self-esteem?

For some people, low self-esteem is a function of deeply rooted, systemic problems that are not likely to be resolved without the help of a skilled therapist. For many others, low self-esteem is due, in large part, to bad mental habits that can be overcome through consciousness and discipline.

Many of us were taught as children that it is not polite to speak highly of ourselves. We got into the habit of putting ourselves down and magnifying our faults, paying a lot more attention to our flaws and the things we don't like about ourselves than to the things that make us feel good about ourselves. Putting attention on something tends to strengthen and reinforce it.

Recognizing your own worth and value is not the same as being conceited. Putting yourself down is not the same as being humble and modest.

Do you constantly make negative pronouncements about yourself, such as, "I have no discipline," "I'm too indecisive," "I hate my voice," etc.? When you make a mistake, do you say, "I'm so dumb," "I have the worst memory," "I always put my foot in my mouth."

Even when you do acknowledge a strength, are you quick to point to the flip side? "I'm creative, that must be why I'm so unorganized."

Okay, you're not perfect. But must you keep dwelling on your imperfections? Even if you don't voice these insecurities, your internal dialogue reinforces them and creates a sense of low self-esteem that comes across to others. If you had a friend who was as critical of you as you are of yourself, you would have broken off the friendship long ago. You wouldn't want to be around someone who constantly pointed out your shortcomings, yet that's what you do to yourself.

Instead of empowering your faults by constantly focusing attention on them, why not emphasize your strengths? I don't mean that you should walk around saying how great you are. Again, it's what you say to yourself that matters most. At the end of this chapter, there are some exercises that can help you convert self-defeating mental habits into self-constructive ones.

These exercises work only if you apply them—a lifelong habit is not broken overnight. You're going to need to monitor your thoughts to make sure that your habit of putting yourself down doesn't creep back in when you're not paying attention. It's going to take discipline and work, but the results will be well worth it.

looks *matter*

One way to feel good about yourself is to look your best. How you look is usually the first thing someone of the opposite sex will notice and respond to about you, and thus is of critical importance. Your appearance can either draw someone to you or keep them from wanting to get any closer.

A lot of people don't think looks should be so important. They think it's inner qualities like kindness, integrity, and intelligence that count—and are what someone should love about them. As true as this may be, it often takes superficial qualities to get people together in the first place. If you wait for someone to be attracted by your inner beauty, you may have a long wait. This may be unfair; nevertheless it is true.

I'm not saying good looks make you a quality person. You can be drop-dead gorgeous, but if there's nothing below the surface, your looks won't keep someone interested. All the outer beauty in the world won't compensate for inner emptiness or ugliness. On the other hand, you may be the most exciting, dynamic, interesting person around, but if no one gets past your appearance, these qualities will be wasted as far as a relationship is concerned.

That you want to look your best doesn't mean you are being vain or narcissistic. Looking good is being gracious to other people, like fixing up your house when you have guests. You clean up and place flowers on the table not to impress them but to make them feel special and to let them know that you care about them.

People tell me they dress for themselves, not for other people. But you don't have to look at yourself. A lot of us are visual and enjoy looking at things that are visually appealing. I love my husband for his kindness, intelligence, and integrity, but I also love the way he looks—just as I would admire a beautiful painting.

The point is not that you have to look like Cindy Crawford or Antonio Banderas to find a relationship, but the better you look, the more people you're going to draw to you—and the more prospects you will have to choose from in finding an appropriate mate. Therefore, it is very important that you present as attractive an appearance as possible.

If you're not blessed with perfect bone structure and the body of an Olympic god, don't worry. I'm not suggesting you should run out and have plastic surgery. With a little effort and a few tricks, anyone can improve their appearance. The shape you're in, the way you take care of yourself, the way you dress, and the way you carry yourself contribute to the overall impression you make.

In my seminars, we spend one evening out of five focusing on looks—clothes, hair, and so on. Clothes can make a huge difference, either positive or negative, in your appearance. You don't have to spend a fortune or have a huge wardrobe to be well dressed. But you do have to put in some time and thought.

Most people are in one of three places about clothes: (1) they have good taste and dress well; (2) they have good taste and don't dress well; (3) they don't have good taste and don't dress well.

If you're in the first group, no action is needed—keep doing what you're doing. If you're in the second group, you probably don't know how to look at yourself objectively or you're stuck in a style that worked for you in the past but doesn't now. A petite, perky woman who dresses as if she were tall and elegant, or a man who is wearing the same hairstyle he wore twenty years ago in college are examples of people in this category. If you're in this group, you need to get some help in order to see yourself better. All you probably need is a little jump start and you'll be fine on your own.

In my experience, people in the third group can either be the easiest or the most difficult to work with. The important thing is to admit that you don't know how to dress. Big deal. No one is good at everything, and the things you are good at are probably much more important. What you need to do is hire or ask someone to help you look your best. Be committed to looking good, not to proving you have a flair for dressing.

My husband is very smart about this. He dresses great because he lets me help him buy his clothes and decide which things go together. Tony knows that he has many great qualities and talents but that good taste in clothes is not one of them.

No matter which category you're in, try to stay current. I'm not talking about being trendy or spending all your free time reading fashion magazines. Just pick one up once in a while.

Daniel was a scientist from Los Alamos Laboratory who took my seminar in Santa Fe, New Mexico. He had a beard covering his face and the kind of sunglasses that are supposed to, but don't, lighten when you go indoors. You could barely see his face. His hair was wild and frizzy and he wore rumpled, ill-fitting clothes. He was a walking ad for Nerd magazine.

The fourth session is usually the one where we work on people's appearance, but he needed immediate help. At the first session I told him to meet me the next day with his credit card. We got him new glasses, a haircut, a shave, and some casual clothes—all for a few hundred dollars. He enjoyed all the attention and realized shopping could be fun with someone who knows how.

At the second session he caused a sensation. We could barely get started because of all the hoopla. People couldn't believe the change in him; several women said they wanted to go out with him. During the next week, a friend of his called me to say that what I had done with Daniel was a miracle. But it really wasn't difficult. All it took were a few "superficial changes" for him to go from being someone whose appearance put people off to someone who was attractive and desirable. Daniel had always been a wonderful guy; the problem was that no one had seen it because they couldn't get past his appearance.

you're never fully dressed *without a* smile

When you smile at someone, you're communicating to them that you are gracious, friendly, and approachable. Just as important, you are communicating those things to yourself.

I first discovered this when I was working as a waitress many years ago. The manager of the restaurant told me to start smiling at people. I protested that it would be phony to smile when I didn't feel like it. He said he didn't care if it was phony, he wanted me to smile. I didn't want to lose the job so I gave it a shot.

At first, I did have to fake it; my smiles were artificial. But after I received a few genuine smiles in response to my fake ones, I started to actually feel happier and more friendly, and my smiles became more spontaneous. The more I smiled, the better time I had, and the more genuine my smiles became. And later, when I counted my tips and discovered they were about 20 percent higher than average, I burst out laughing.

A woman named Carol approached me one night in Cleveland where I was leading my seminar. She said she was a doctor and made a lot of money. She drove an expensive car and wore expensive clothes. She said men either were intimidated by her or wanted her for her money. She was sick of this and didn't think she should have to hide her success to find a relationship.

I said I was sure she was justified in everything she said, and asked if I could share an observation. I told her that she came across as critical, cynical, and angry, and that I thought that might be the problem. I suggested that smiling a lot might help her change her demeanor.

She was taken aback, but what I said sank in. She had been told once before that she had a chip on her shoulder about men, and she wanted to change that. When she returned the following week she was much softer. She said she felt less uptight and her friends had noticed a change in her as well. She also thought that men were responding to her differently.

You will probably find yourself becoming a friendlier, more open, and more cheerful person as a result of smiling at people, but that's only a side benefit. The main reason for doing it is that when you smile at people you make it much easier for them to start a conversation with you, and more of them will do so.

Maybe you think you're too shy to smile. It is, however, a proven fact that it is physiologically possible for shy people to smile—you don't have to wait until your personality changes.

"What if people think I'm coming on to them," you ask. You are—that's the point. You can handle it if someone mistakes your smile for a come-on. Better you should have to fend off a few people you don't want to meet than to miss out on meeting someone you do.

I can't tell you how many couples first got together because one of them smiled. That's how I met my husband, Tony. Actually, I was smiling at the guy standing next to him, but my aim must have been off. The other guy ignored me, but Tony came over and started a conversation. Later, when I asked him why he approached me, he said it was because I had smiled at him. The power of a smile to make someone feel comfortable was reinforced for me after I got to know Tony and discovered how shy he is.

The more attractive you are, the more likely it is that someone will feel intimidated about approaching you. A lot of people automatically assume that someone who is really good-looking is not available or wouldn't be interested in them. I've met quite a few gorgeous women who didn't realize that was the reason men weren't asking them out. If you're very attractive, you should smile even more.

step 4 assignments

1. Smile and say hello to fifty people a week.

The way to approach this is to make it a game and really go for it. Don't say, "I work at home; I don't see that many people in a week." The idea here is that to reach your quota of fifty smiles and hellos within one week, you're going to have to go to places where you will see members of the opposite sex.

Those places exist in everyday life. You will find you can spot people to smile at while standing in line at the bank or the post office, on an elevator, buying a latte or a newspaper, or at the dry cleaner or car wash.

Margaret, who took my course in Seattle last year, woke up on Sunday morning realizing she had forty smiles left to do before the "deadline" on the next night.

She positioned herself at the finish line of the Seattle marathon and smiled at the runners as they finished the race. (Besides being an efficient way to complete the assignment, it helped alleviate Margaret's concerns about safety. She figured someone who had just run 26.2 miles would not be likely to hassle her.)

To her delight, both men and women came up to thank her for being there, and to tell her how much her smiles had encouraged and supported them. She not only went over her quota of fifty smiles, she is presently married to one of those runners.

So don't be surprised if some outrageous things start to happen.

Even though I'm married, I still smile at people. It's how I meet interesting people all over the world.

Participants in my seminars often complain that people don't return their smiles or make eye contact. Not everyone will—and that's okay. The point of this exercise is not for you to *get* fifty smiles but to *give* them. Why do you think I set the number at fifty? That way, even if the majority don't respond, you'll still probably end up meeting one or two people. And if you do, this exercise will have been a success.

Occasionally, women will express concerns about the dangers involved in smiling at men. Some places are better than others for meeting members of the opposite sex (see the lists on page 67).

2. List ten qualities that make you a great catch. Ask yourself, "What special and unique attributes do I bring to a relationship?" If you can't come up with a complete list, ask your friends to help you.

3. Assess your appearance and wardrobe. Get help from your support person or from someone who has good taste and whom you can trust to be honest with you. Use the Appearance Checklist to evaluate which aspects of your appearance are working for you and which aren't.

Appearance Checklist

	ACTION (*if needed*)	*	BY WHEN
Hair			
Skin			
Teeth			
Weight			
Exercise			
Clothing			
for work			
for play			
for dating			
accessories (shoes, belts, jewelry)			
Eyewear (glasses, contacts)			
FOR WOMEN:			
makeup			
nails			
FOR MEN:			
facial hair			

4. Purge your closet.

Wearing clothes in which you do not feel attractive diminishes your self-esteem. If you're like most people, you're happy with only about half the clothes in your closet. The remaining items are "things that might come back into style," "bargains," and the forty-three old shirts you're keeping to wear next time you paint.

Each time you bought a pair of pants, a sweater, or a skirt on sale, you probably said, "For $30 I can't go wrong." But guess what. You've gone wrong twenty times for $30.

It's time to clear out everything in your closet that does not help you look and feel your best.

If you're like most people, you're going to need help on this one. Remember: You're the one who got yourself into this mess in the first place. Pick someone who will be ruthless in forcing you to get rid of anything that doesn't make you look your best.

5. Complete the following sentences:

I am waiting until I'm married or in a relationship to:
Have (e.g., a home, insurance, investments):

Do (e.g., travel, learn to ski):

Feel (e.g., successful, adventurous):

get out there and date

d on't worry. I'm not going to try to convince you that dating is fun. I know how horrible it can be. But it works. Dating leads to relationships. Dating is a numbers game: The more people you go out with, the greater your chances of finding someone with whom you really connect.

The advice, rules, dos, and don'ts of this chapter are based on my experiences with thousands of single people. This is a dating survival guide that will allow you to avoid their mistakes and move from dating to a relationship with as little wear and tear as possible.

RULE #1: JUST DO IT

If your goal was to become vice-president of your company, you wouldn't say, "No way I'm going anywhere near a client meeting," or "I refuse to meet with the sales team." If you planned on becoming a concert pianist, you wouldn't say, "I don't have time to practice," or "I won't play scales." If you wanted to be an Olympic swimmer, you wouldn't say, "I don't want to get my hair wet."

But you, a single person whose goal is to be in a relationship, say things like: "I want a relationship but I don't like the dating scene."

If I knew exactly when and where you would meet the person who is perfect for you, we would have charged a lot more for this book. There's no way around it: You're going to have to bite the bullet and go on dates. Lot of dates.

Salespeople know that not every prospect turns into a customer, so they call on prospect after prospect. They consider themselves successful if one out of every dozen signs an order.

Fortunately, there are a variety of resources, including personal ads, dating services, and your personal network to help you in your quest for people to date. Later in this chapter there are tips for making the most of these resources.

RULE # 2: DON'T BE A SNOB

People always tell me that they know they would never be interested in someone who would hang out at a bar, join a dating service, or go on a blind date. I tell them they're wrong. Dating is not about limiting options but expanding them.

Two of the biggest mistakes you can make in looking for a relationship are thinking you know which people are your "type," and thinking you know where you will meet them. This myth is so disastrous I've devoted an entire chapter to it (the step 6 chapter).

good place to meet people. His attitude was that even though he wasn't interested in cooking, he did like to eat. His dinner party invitations skyrocketed after the class, and now he knows how to whip up snacks that make him happier than the cheese sandwiches and hot dogs that were his steady diet before.

My friend Stan asked me where I thought he could meet some interesting women. I told him to get involved in the arts, something he had no particular interest in at the time. He got on the board of a local ballet company in his city. He called me after the first meeting, distressed because the other board members were all married women. I said, "Don't worry, Stan, they'll take care of you." And they did—he's now married to one of their daughters. But he continues to work on the board because it gives him tremendous satisfaction.

If you aren't willing to do anything or go anywhere to meet people, I have one piece of advice: Pray. In fact, why not go to church or synagogue or to a Quaker meeting. You just might meet people who share your faith.

RULE # 6: BE PERSONAL

Once you meet people, it's important to actually get to know them, which is not the same as spending time with them. Small talk is fun and a good way to get familiar with someone's personality, but you should try to create an opening for deeper conversation as well.

This is another aspect of relationships that we were much better at when we were in school. In college, you could meet someone at a party and feel like you were close friends by the next day. It wasn't unusual back then to stay up half the night with someone you'd just met, getting to know each other.

But as you got older, you became more concerned with the outcome of relationships, with where they were going, and less interested in being with someone just for the sake of sharing experiences.

To get personal with someone, you have to learn how to become a good interviewer. Normally, when you interview people you've just met, you ask them what their job is, where they grew up, where they like to go skiing, what restaurants they enjoy, and so on. You discuss the wrapping and never get inside the package. Questions like these help you discover whether someone fits into your lifestyle, not what he or she is really like.

At the end of this chapter you'll find a list of "ice-breaking" questions that will help open the way for deeper communication. The spirit in which you ask these questions is as important as the questions themselves. This is not about probing into people's private lives or interrogating them about how many kids they plan to have. You're not interviewing people for the job of "prospective spouse." You're just trying to get to know them.

If you're not genuinely interested in someone, try pretending that you are. Just like when my fake smiles turned into real ones, you may find you actually do become interested.

The key is to listen. Also, since it's a rare person whose favorite subject isn't him- or herself, don't be surprised if your interest in this subject makes your date think you're fascinating.

By getting personal with the people you date, you'll help ensure that you don't let "the one" slip through your fingers. When you do eliminate someone, your decision will be an informed one. You'll know who it is you're passing up.

RULE # 7: DON'T HUNT IN A PACK

Avoid going out with more than one friend; a pack of men or women tends to be intimidating. Better yet, go out by yourself. You'll be more focused on meeting people and will seem more available and approachable. Also, you won't have to worry about someone else's opinions. It's hard enough to meet someone new without your friend saying, "How could you be interested in her?" or "I can't believe you flirted with every guy at the bar."

If you do go out with a friend, be sure to make it clear that this outing is part of your project. Make sure he or she supports your goal of meeting people.

in defense *of bars*

Many singles think the only people in bars are heavy drinkers. Yes, there are people who go to bars just to get drunk or to find a one-night stand. But there are many others who go to bars to meet people like you. You may have to do some research to find out which bars in your city are frequented by the kind of people you'd like to meet.

People who know us think it's funny that I met my husband in a bar because neither of us drink. If you haven't been to any bars lately, you might be surprised at the number of soft drinks and bottled waters being consumed in many of them.

When you go to a bar (or anywhere else), be up front with people about what you're doing there. I remember being asked on several occasions, "What's an intelligent, good-looking woman like you doing in a bar?" I would answer, "I'm here to meet someone," or "I'm here to fall in love with someone. What are you doing here?"

dating dos and don'ts

FOR MEN ONLY

Do ask women out. Men have stopped doing this. I ask them what they're waiting for and they say they're waiting to get over their divorce, until they're not feeling shy, until they lose weight or handle their business or until their kids are grown or college is paid for.

Most of all, they're waiting for a sure thing. They don't want to ask a woman out unless they're sure she will accept. They don't want to risk going out with anyone unless they're sure they can have a failure-proof relationship. It's like refusing to buy a pair of running shoes unless it's guaranteed you'll finish a marathon.

Men, if you want a relationship, you're going to have to get over your fear of failure. Take the risk and ask women out.

Do be specific. Invite her to a specific event at a specific time. For example, "Would you like to go to dinner Wednesday night," not "Would you like to go out sometime?"

Do have a plan. Choose the restaurant in advance and make a reservation if one is needed.

Don't ask her to pay for herself when you go out. It's really tacky. If you can't or don't want to spend a lot of money, go on dates that cost nothing or very little. Take her out for coffee, to a museum or art exhibit, or on a walk—but take her out.

Why? Because it's gracious. Because women like it. Most of us would prefer to go out *on* a cheap date than *with* a cheap date.

If a woman offers to pay, it's okay to accept. But don't

ever ask her to pay. Don't say, "I've taken you out four times. I think it's your turn."

Don't give a woman your card and say, "Call me." This is something women really hate.

Men do this to avoid rejection. If you ask a woman for her number and she asks you for your card, then it's okay to give it to her. But it's rude to expect her to be the one to call.

Don't ask a woman for her number and not call her. What's the matter with you? I still haven't figured out why men do this; it must be something on the Y chromosome, like the inability to ask for directions.

If you know you're not going to call her, don't ask for her number. If you ask for her number, call her. If you ask for her number and don't call her, you will justifiably be regarded as a jerk.

Hint: Put her name on the piece of paper with her number. I have this vision of men's bureaus filled with stacks of matchbook covers with phone numbers scribbled on them and no names.

FOR WOMEN ONLY

Don't ask men out. Most of them don't respond well to this. Even though many things about relationships have changed in recent years, there is still a courting etiquette that dictates that the man ask the woman out. Just as it would make most men uncomfortable if you went around opening doors for them, asking them out can get things off to an awkward start.

This is true even for men who *say* they like it when women ask them out. They think they like it because it keeps them from having to feel rejected, but at the same time, it makes them nervous. The way around this is to tell a man you'd like him to ask you out. This approach allows you to have your cake and eat it, too.

Do be clear about letting men know you're interested. Instead of relying on body language to convey your interest, use English. Be direct. For example, you could say, "I enjoyed talking to you. I'd really love it if you asked me out."

Women, this really works. Men are becoming increasingly risk-aversive, and many of them simply will not ask a woman out unless they know in advance she will not reject them. You may find this embarrassing at first, but you will be amazed at the results you'll get.

Do offer to pay on a date, but only if you feel comfortable doing so. Don't insist, however, if he declines your offer. Another way to reciprocate is to invite him over for dinner.

FOR SINGLE PARENTS

Many single parents have told me they feel dating is more difficult for them. They're right: Each person you add to a relationship makes it more complicated and complex. However, being a parent does not have to prevent you from finding a relationship.

Even though your children are your priority, you need to make time for yourself and for having a relationship. Besides, doing so will have a positive impact on your well-being, which can only benefit your children. I recommend you set aside one night a week for this purpose. Stop using your kids as an excuse. Surely you can find someone to take care of them; we're only talking about one night a week.

Don't bring your children into the relationship until it is a relationship. Don't say, "I'm a package deal so anyone who dates me has got to know my children and vice versa." I'm not suggesting that you should hide your children or lie about the fact that you are a parent, just that you establish your relationship before bringing them into it. In the beginning, a relationship is fragile. Only after you build a strong foundation—by getting to know each other and establishing intimacy and trust—can a relationship withstand the strain children tend to put on it.

But protecting the relationship is not the most important reason for this advice. It is not to your children's benefit to expose them to relationships that are not established and secure. If the relationship breaks up, the child will always lose. If your child likes the person you're dating, it can engender hopes, expectation, and attachment, which can lead to feelings of loss and disappointment if you break up. If your child doesn't like the person you're dating, it can be a difficult and frustrating experience for them, one that you shouldn't put them through unnecessarily.

FOR PEOPLE DATING A SINGLE PARENT

Contrary to popular opinion, you don't have to like his or her children and they don't have to like you in order for the two of you to have a relationship. It may take time for your relationship with his or her kids to develop, and it may never be wonderful. Workable is sufficient.

It's important to be clear with the children (and with yourself) that you aren't trying to replace their parent. Also, don't try to parent another person's child and don't offer unsolicited advice about parenting, even if you think you know best. Stay out—this is a real source of problems in many relationships. That doesn't mean you can't establish limits or ground rules for how the children behave when they're with you. Just don't try to set them for anyone else.

If you both have kids, things can definitely get complicated. There are professional counselors who specialize in dealing with the problems that frequently occur in "blended" families. If you're experiencing difficulties, don't wait to seek out this kind of help. By getting support earlier rather than later, you can learn skills that will help you get past the challenges of this situation and prevent a lot of pain.

dating resources

In most cities, personal ads, on-line networking, dating services, and singles' groups, clubs, and events abound. Like with most other things, what you get out of these resources will depend on what you put into them. Just joining an organization or placing an ad isn't enough; you have to actually show up for events and make an effort to meet the people who are there.

The purpose of these resources is to create a flow of new people into your life, not to qualify and screen them (we'll work on screening techniques in the step 6 chapter).

PERSONAL ADS

✴ *placing an ad.* Start by selecting one or more publications for your ad. You can approach this as though you were a business advertiser and find out from various publications what their demographics are, or just choose a newspaper or magazine you like to read.

It's a good idea to read a bunch of ads to get a feel for

them. Notice the length, content, and style of those you like and use them as a guide when you write your own.

The biggest mistake people make in writing personal ads is listing too many criteria designed to screen people out. It's okay to mention some things you are looking for, but don't overdo it. The goal is to generate the maximum number of new prospects. The time to screen for quality is after you meet the respondents, not before.

✳ *answering an ad*. The key to handling the responses to your ad is to answer all of them (with the exception of obvious creeps).

Lawrence did not have the benefit of this advice when he placed his personal ad, a few weeks before he took my seminar. He separated his forty-five responses into a "good" pile and a "reject" pile. Seven women made it into the good pile; there were thirty-eight rejects. He began phoning the good ones. The first got disqualified on the telephone and the second rejected him after three promising dates. After this rejection, he didn't feel like calling anyone else.

During my seminar, he realized that he had been overdoing it a bit with the criteria he was using to screen women out. He saw that he hadn't given the respondents enough of a chance.

He went through his two piles again. This time, only three women landed in the reject stack. He began calling the remaining respondents one by one until, midway through the pile, he met a woman he really liked. He ended up marrying her later that year. They still laugh about the fact that she was originally "Reject #19."

Use your imagination. An ad Vicki read captured her

interest because she found it clever and humorous. The writer jokingly said, "Nude photographs will be looked upon favorably." Vicki sent him a photograph of a Picasso nude with a funny note. Impressed with her sense of humor, he called her. They have been going together for six months.

* *arranging a meeting.* Whether you answer an ad or someone answers yours, one thing to avoid is an extended initial telephone conversation. After talking with someone for three hours on the phone, it can feel anticlimactic when you meet for a date. Try not to stay on the phone for more than ten or fifteen minutes.

If you have a positive reaction to someone on the phone, see if you can arrange a time and place to meet. It's usually best to meet at a public place like a coffeehouse, restaurant, or park. While I like the idea of men picking women up at their home when you go on a date, I don't advise this for the first time you meet someone from an ad.

ON-LINE NETWORKING

Meeting people on the Internet is fun but impractical for your purposes, since the odds are against you connecting with people who live near you. Instead, research local bulletin boards, chat lines, and user groups that provide a "place" where you can connect to other singles with modems.

Try logging on at different times of the day and week. Once you've connected with someone you find interesting, don't wait too long to meet her or him in person. Otherwise, you can end up investing a lot of time and energy into what amounts to an imaginary relationship when you should be getting involved with flesh-and-blood people.

DATING SERVICES

I can't tell you how many people have come to my seminars complaining that they "tried a dating service" and didn't meet anyone. After a little probing, the truth always came out. They had submitted their video and waited for someone to discover them. This is like joining a gym and never going to work out, then complaining that it didn't help you get in shape. After my seminar, some of these same people went back to the services they had joined. They got to work reviewing the videos of the other members and making contact with them. Of course, they got results.

Don't be put off by the high fees some dating services charge. It's usually possible to negotiate a lower fee. Try it.

Remember, the purpose of these dating resources is to increase the flow of people into your life. Use them to connect with as many people as possible.

step 5 assignments

1. Continue to smile and say hello to fifty people a week.

2. Conduct a personal interview.

  Use the "ice-breaking questions" on page 71 as a guideline. You can do this with someone you're dating or, if this is too frightening, with a friend.

3. Research dating services in your area.

  Find out how they operate: Do they use videos, personal interviews, or actual matchmaking? Consider which approaches would be most comfortable for you. Inquire about the different programs they offer and compare costs. Check out some of their tapes or profiles. Ask for references.

4. Research local on-line services.

Using the above guidelines, explore options for connecting with people in your area via modem. Inquire about free trials.

5. Respond to a personal ad.

Read ads in different local publications until you find one that appeals to you. Answer one or more ads.

6. Write and place a personal ad.

Using ads you like as a reference, write your own ad and place it in a local publication. If you don't get many responses, don't take it personally. Take it as an indication that your ad was ineffective and write another one.

7. Join a club, sign up for a class, or get involved in a new activity in which there is a likelihood of meeting members of the opposite sex.

8. Ask five friends to support you by fixing you up and remembering to think of you for parties and other activities. Tell them you just want to start going out and meeting some new people, that they don't have to be responsible for finding the perfect match for you. Most important, if they do fix you up, don't criticize their choice. Don't say, "What were you thinking," or "Thanks a lot for the creep you set me up with." If you do, don't expect them to ever fix you up again.

9. Make a promise to your support person about a specific action you will take this week to advance your search for a relationship.

10. Get a date.

Women: Tell a man you're interested in him and would like him to ask you out. Do this with as many men as necessary until one of them takes the bait.

Men: Ask as many women out as necessary until one of them accepts.

places to meet people

attend sporting events:

* golf tournaments
* tennis matches
* basketball, baseball, or football games

participate in athletic activities:

* softball
* volleyball
* aerobics or health club
* triathlon training club
* sailing or windsurfing
* jogging club
* martial arts
* skiing, especially with an organized ski club
* horseback riding
* bicycling club
* hiking or mountaineering club
* swimming or scuba diving
* river rafting
* dance classes (ballroom, country western, salsa, etc.)

take a course:

  * boating
  * art appreciation
  * fly-fishing
  * investments
  * carpentry
  * painting
  * photography
  * cooking
  * needlepoint
  * weaving
  * language lessons

shop in:

  * grocery stores, especially on "Singles' Night" (if available)
  * men's/women's stores
  * bookstores
  * sporting goods stores
  * computer stores
  * cosmetic counters
  * wine shops
  * camera shops
  * hardware stores
  * car dealerships

attend cultural events:

  * gallery openings
  * plays (including the discussion groups)
  * museums

volunteer:

* in a hospital
* to help a political candidate
* at a public television station
* as a tour guide
* in an art museum
* to participate in a fund-raising event
* to collect for a charity
* for a tournament sport

hang out at:

* racetracks
* marinas
* auctions
* libraries
* coffeehouses
* museums
* AA meetings
* car washes

and:

* travel alone or go on a singles' trip
* go to bars during "Happy Hour"
* join or start a singles' dinner group
* eat breakfast out alone near business places
* visit the zoo (many single parents are there with kids)
* take a ferry ride
* take your niece or nephew to the park
* teach a class or workshop

* go to trade shows
* join a choir or singing group
* go to singles' events
* attend religious services
* go to political events or party meetings
* connect through local on-line singles' bulletin boards:
* connect in line (at movies, grocery stores, banks, etc.)

for men: ten good places to meet women:

1. Get involved in the arts

2. Cooking classes

3. Arts and crafts classes

4. Fashion shows

5. Horse shows

6. Aerobics classes

7. Yoga classes

8. Cosmetic counters

9. Dance classes

10. Garden clubs and tours

for women: ten good places to meet men:

1. Golf courses or driving ranges

2. Computer stores

3. Hardware stores

4. Car auctions or rallies

5. Auto supply stores

6. Sporting events

7. Fly-fishing classes

8. Boat shows

9. Skeet-shooting classes

10. Political events

ice-breaking questions:

1. What kind of work do you do?
   What do you love about it?
   What about it challenges you the most?
   What about it frustrates you the most?
   What is your dream regarding your work?

2. What have been the major accomplishments of your life so far?
   What do you consider your biggest failure?

3. What are you most passionate about?
   Where did this interest come from?

4. What's the best thing that's happened to you in the last year?
   What's the worst thing?

5. What would you do if you didn't have to work?

6. Describe your ideal vacation.

7. Would you like to be famous?
   If yes, what would you like to be famous for?

If not, why not?

(If they are famous) What do you like/dislike about being famous?

8. If you were given $20 million tomorrow, what would you do with it?

9. What was it like growing up in your family?
   What good qualities do you attribute to your upbringing?
   What bad qualities do you attribute to your upbringing?

10. Describe what kind of relationship you want.

11. Are you romantic?
    If yes, in what way(s)?

12. How do you think men are different from women?

13. What makes you happy?

14. What makes you sad?

15. What were you like as a child?

16. As a child, what did you want to be when you grew up?
    As an adult, what do you want to be when you grow up?

17. What do you think makes you different from other people?

18. Do you believe in God?
    What is your concept of her/him?

19. To what extent do you feel your actions as an individual can affect social change?

20. What do you consider the three most important social issues today?
    What would you do about them if you could?

21. What do you love about your life?

22. What are the milestones in your life? The important turning points?

23. What do you complain about? What are your pet peeves?

You can add any questions you'd like to this list. What do you really want to know about someone? Just ask.

step **6**

just say yes

Reading this book may help you learn how to make yourself more attractive or more available or to get out there and date. But there's one area where you know you don't need coaching. You are absolutely, 100 percent sure you know "your type."

Wrong!

One of the biggest mistakes you can make in your quest for a lifetime mate is believing you know which people are your type. An even bigger mistake is thinking you know which ones aren't.

I used to think I knew. One night, about four months after I moved to Seattle, I was sitting at Duke's Bar and Grill. There were a lot of men there but none of them were my type. I finished my third Diet Pepsi and decided to call it quits for the night.

Just then, a group of Sonics (Seattle's basketball team) walked into the bar. I noticed they were all tall, athletic, self-assured, and powerful men—in other words, my type!

I was trying to figure out how to meet one of these

exciting guys when a boring corporate-looking man in a suit came up and introduced himself as Tony. We talked for a few minutes and he invited me to join him and the team at a party they were having upstairs. Perfect, I thought, here's my opportunity to meet the players.

It turned out Tony was an executive with the team. He was mild-mannered and reserved—definitely not my type. But since he was my entrée to those who were, I stuck around.

That night he invited me to go to the final game of the season and to the banquet that followed. I accepted again, callous as it was, not because I was interested in Tony but because I wanted to hang out with the team. When he took me home that night I made it clear I was not interested in him.

A couple of days later I woke up with a terrible neckache. I lay there in excruciating pain—crying and unable to move—when the phone rang. It was Tony. He apparently wasn't letting my rejection stop him. I told him about my neck and he quickly got me in to see the team doctor. Afterward he took me to lunch, then got me the medicine I needed.

Even though I still wasn't interested in him romantically, I really appreciated how kind he had been, so I invited him to dinner the next night.

That night he asked me out for the following evening. I enjoyed his company, but he just wasn't my type. He was too quiet, shy, and "nice"—not powerful and exciting enough.

I accepted his invitation for the next night, planning to tell him then that I didn't think we should see each other any more. But I ended up having such a good time that I accepted another date. After two weeks of seeing him almost every night, I was in love.

I ruled Tony out as a possible mate when I first met him because I had a very narrow "screening" system based on a strict list of characteristics that added up to what I believed was my type. I dismissed him because I didn't have that gut feeling I got when I was with men I thought were exciting and powerful.

It took me two weeks to get beyond the superficial qualities I found unattractive in Tony. Once I got to know him better, I realized the quietness I had interpreted as weakness was actually more powerful than the kind of forceful machismo I had always equated with strength. I discovered that he had a great sense of humor and that he was sensitive and intelligent. I'd been looking so hard for indications of my "type," I had missed most of Tony's best qualities. And the more I got to know him, the more I realized how perfect he was for me.

The truth is, you've found your type over and over again. You've gone out with them, lived with them, maybe even married them. But the relationships just haven't worked out. That's because you don't really know your type, you just think you do.

Why are so many intelligent, successful people clueless about their type? It's because they place an inappropriate emphasis on initial chemistry.

You meet someone at a party and right away you click. You like the way she wears her hair or you like his voice. Something you can't quite put your finger on triggers a positive gut reaction. You know that magic feeling—it's chemistry.

It may be easier to understand this type of chemistry if you know where it comes from. It all started with cavemen: In order to survive, primitive people required mates. "He" needed a "she" who could make lots of cavebabies and keep the home fires burning. "She" was looking for a "he" who would fend off saber-toothed tigers and drag home dinner. It was pretty much, you take care of me and I'll take care of you and together we'll keep this whole species thing going. There wasn't a whole lot of talk about feelings.

Given the reasons for mating, the best bets among the females were the wide-hipped women who looked like they could drop a baby at noon and still get dinner on the table. Among the males they were the men known for their hunting skills—the ones you could count on to drag home a woolly mammoth instead of a measly rabbit.

Over the years, a survival instinct developed that triggered a positive response and the release of pheromones whenever a man spotted a fertile-looking woman or a woman bumped into a guy with a cave full of pelts. The cavemen successfully mounted and mated, the species evolved, and the survival mechanism filtered down through the ages, generally causing men to rate women by their looks and women to evaluate men by what they did. I call it the "rich man, sexy woman" formula, and it is the basis for what we call chemistry.

The gut reaction you think is a personal indicator of your soulmate is actually a deep-seated survival mechanism that hasn't changed much in the last forty thousand years—about as personal to you as getting up on two feet instead of four.

What if I told you women I wanted to introduce you to a short man in his late forties with a big nose, thick glasses, and ears that stick out? Sound interesting? What if I told you his name was Steven Spielberg? Notice a shift in attitude? In chemistry quotient?

Now I bring in a hunk—tall, gorgeous, classic, sexy. I introduce you to Frank, a male dancer who strips for a living.

Not interested, right? No need for discussion, you know he's not your type. Might be okay for one night if you're really horny, but based purely on his "profession," you have ruled him out as a possible relationship.

Next, I introduce the men to a real knockout. An exquisite woman with flawless skin, gorgeous hair, and a perfect body. Her name is Patti and she sells doughnuts in the mall. "So?" you reply. "She's employed; I'm no snob."

Really? Meet Rene, an extraordinary woman, a famous heart surgeon. People come from all over the world to study her surgical techniques. She's also an expert mountain climber, has scaled all the major peaks in North America and others throughout the world. She's average-looking—not ugly but has heavy calves and thighs.

What? No takers? Maybe someone would like to get some information from her about a climbing expedition, but "Where is that doughnut lady you were telling me about?"

For men, chemistry is still largely based on what a woman looks like; for women, it's still what a man does. The "rich man, sexy woman" syndrome remains intact despite thousands of years of history.

Everyone's pissed off about this. Women complain that men only care about the size of their breasts and their percentage of body fat. And men think that women only care about the size of their wallets. But being angry about chemistry is like being mad about the rain in Seattle—that's just the way it is.

Using chemistry as a method of choosing a mate was viable up until very recently. When most of our parents got together, women needed men to survive financially. Very few women worked outside the home. By definition, a good husband was a good provider. Not so obvious was the fact that a man needed a wife as an entrée into society. He could not rise on the corporate ladder, run for political office, or be a respected member of the community without a wife. And not just any wife—she needed to look and act the part. A wife's demeanor could make or break a man's career.

Practically overnight, the reasons for mating have changed. For the most part, women don't need men to survive. And men no longer need a wife to ensure their career advancement.

The functional requirements for mating have for the most part been supplanted by psychological or emotional needs. Now people are seeking a sense of security and belonging. They want intimacy, someone with whom to share their lives.

These needs were once met by extended families and the community. My mother used to talk to her mother every day about the kids or what she was cooking for dinner. She had coffee with the next-door neighbor nearly every morning. My father went to the "health club" every day after work. His "workout" consisted of playing poker and smoking cigars. This was where he went to discuss business and argue sports and politics with the guys.

Now families live in separate cities, in distant states. I'm proud that I even know my neighbors' names. And the only bonding at a health club is between you and the Stairmaster.

Today, we look to our primary partner to be someone we can talk to about the kids, our work, how we feel about things, and what to have for dinner. We want deep, passionate relationships. We want someone we can talk to and with whom we can laugh and be intimate. Yet we keep going for people with whom we have chemistry. When it comes to evaluating a potential Mr. or Ms. Right, we ask, "How small is her waist?" or "Where does he live?"

Most of us have a double standard. We want to be judged by what really matters—the deep, meaningful qualities that make us worthwhile people—but that's not how we judge others.

A man I know told me he was sick of unsatisfying relationships, that he really wanted to meet a woman of substance, someone who was loving, considerate, and spiritual. I suggested he run a personal ad. He thought that was a great idea and placed one the following week—in which he advertised for a "redhead, 5′6″ and thin."

This man really did want a sensitive woman and an emotionally fulfilling relationship, but he was using criteria designed to help him find a functional one.

It's chemistry that makes most of you decide if someone is or isn't "your type." There's nothing wrong with chemistry, but its value is limited. If you feel it, go ahead—enjoy it. Flirt all you want. But don't take it too seriously and please don't use it as an indicator of whether a relationship will succeed in the long term. An initial positive gut reaction doesn't mean you're going to have a good relationship with someone, nor does an initially neutral or even negative reaction mean you won't.

Any connection between your first reaction and what develops in a relationship is probably nothing more than coincidence. If you've ever been involved with someone where you had great chemistry only to find there was nothing to keep you together after the initial buzz wore off, you know what I'm talking about.

What about "love at first sight?" Or your cousin Vera and her husband, who have a terrific marriage and knew right away that they were meant for each other? It's true, it happens.

But consider this: In my course, I give an assignment to interview two happily married couples about their relationships and specifically about their initial encounters. So far the participants have interviewed more than two thousand couples. I'm not talking about two thousand couples who tolerate each other or stay together because it's comfortable. I'm talking about two thousand couples in long-term, deeply passionate relationships. And guess what? When asked if they had any chemistry when they first met, 90 percent of these couples answered no!

So, to use initial chemistry as your sole indicator of whether you should pursue someone as a relationship candidate is ridiculous. Would you invest your money in a venture that had only a 10 percent chance of success?

Still, a lot of people can't resist a long shot. If they get that "magic feeling," they're off and running. It's not surprising. When you experience chemistry with someone, you like them right away. It's easy to connect. Flirting feels natural. You're eager to get to know them better. All you have to do is let nature take its course, and before you know it—you're "involved."

When there's no chemistry, it's a real "catch-22." You aren't motivated to get to know the person better, yet it's only by getting to know someone better that you'll discover whether or not there's a real bond between you.

Does this mean you should avoid someone with whom you have initial chemistry? Absolutely not. If you feel an immediate spark, by all means, get to know him or her better. But you should also try to get to know people with whom you don't feel initial chemistry. By giving someone you don't think is your type a chance, you may discover, as I did with Tony, that there is an attraction between you that is slower to build but every bit as passionate. This is the kind of chemistry that can last forever.

beyond chemical dependency

In my seminars, I tell people to become "talent scouts." The job of a talent scout is to find a star before he or she has become one. There's no money in discovering somebody who's already been discovered. What you've been doing is going for the glitz, for people who are already shining. And you've probably found that they're already taken or that they don't live up to their initial promise.

Let's say you're a single man. You go to a party. There are ten available women there. Two of them shine. Two of them bark. You approach the beauties, carefully avoiding the dogs. One of them snubs you; the other one leaves with a Brad Pitt look-alike. Asked the next day how the party was, you say, "Okay, but there was only one good woman there and she left before I had a chance to talk to her."

I say there were six women there you never even saw. One, maybe even two or three of them, were true beauties. You dismissed them because their beauty was not immediately apparent. Even Sharon Stone could go unnoticed at a party if she were dressed down and not made up. And if you could miss even outer beauty because you didn't look hard enough, think of all the inner beauty that's escaping you.

We've all had the experience of meeting people who we think are hot only to have that impression reversed when they open their mouth. The opposite also happens. We meet people and have no immediate chemistry, but after spending a little time with them we start to feel a physical attraction.

Stars are made, not born—and we all have the power to

help make people into stars. When she began her career, Julia Roberts was not considered an incredible beauty—just a cute, appealing girl. Tom Cruise was in several movies before he became a sex symbol. Many people become better-looking when we get to know them. And people tend to blossom when they are happy and nurtured, as they are when they're in good relationships.

What I'm suggesting is that you should give people more time before you decide to reject them. If you decide at the end of the first date that he or she is "nice but not your type," I strongly suggest you employ the Nita Tucker Three-Date Rule.

Unless a person is crude, rude, or steals your silverware, try to reserve judgment until you've gone on at least three dates. If I hadn't followed this advice (albeit unwittingly), I would not be married today.

I can hear you now, whining that I'm telling you to waste your time or to compromise, to be with someone you find physically unattractive.

I am not telling you to settle or proposing that you lower your standards. And I'm not saying you should have a relationship with someone you find physically repulsive. I think sexual attraction is critically important. I'm simply suggesting that you invest a few more hours and get to know the person better. It's hard to tell right off the bat how attracted you really are to someone. It's not that your expectations are too high, it's just that they're inaccurate.

Ten years of feedback from people who have taken my seminars indicates that the three-date rule made the biggest difference in their dating experiences, and many people claim if they hadn't followed it they would never have connected with their mates.

One of these people is a stunning woman I know in L.A. who complained to me about the lack of romance in her life. "I get asked out all the time," she told me. "That's not the problem. The problem is I can't seem to find anyone I'm interested in seeing again after the first date. There are just no good men around."

My antenna went up. I recommended she apply the three-date rule. She went out again, and at the end of the evening she had the same old feelings of indifference, but she made a second date because she had agreed to try the rule. To her surprise, after the second date she thought the guy was cute. After the third date, very cute.

She told me—after about their fifth date—that she'd never met a more interesting man. I pointed out that she'd never given a man that kind of chance before. She, like many of you, was too good at screening people out.

So what if you go out with someone three times and, God forbid, it doesn't turn into a passionate lifetime relationship? I know you'd rather spend your precious time reading a book. But spending time with people, finding out what their dreams are, what their life is like . . . that's the stuff the books you'd rather be reading are made of.

I attended a weekend party several years ago at a beautiful island home. There were quite a few single men there as well as single women.

On the first day, I was sitting around talking with some of the women. They were discussing how disappointed they were that there weren't more single men.

"I noticed a lot of single men," I said.

"Yeah, but they're all engineers," they responded. "You know engineers."

"No, I don't know engineers," I said. "Maybe you should give these guys more of a chance."

But, no, these men were boring engineers who didn't know how to dress and weren't good-looking enough.

These women might have made up their minds but I hadn't. I wanted to find out more about the men at the party, so I struck up conversations with all of them.

One had traveled all over the world skiing, and when he talked about his love of nature and his commitment to challenging himself, I was enthralled. Another told me about a water-powered device he'd invented, and it was the most lucid scientific explanation I had ever heard. His hobby was designing and building houses. Another was a pilot who collected planes and helicopters. Another trained racehorses. In other words, this was an amazing group of men.

Naturally, I reported back about these "finds" to the women who had rebuffed them. It turned out they weren't as dumb as I thought. Once they realized how interesting these "boring engineers" were, they beat a path to them. If I hadn't been there to help them get beyond their first impressions, those women would still be saying, "It was a beautiful island, a lovely home, a nice party. But there just weren't any men."

All of us operate with a strict set of unwritten rules and guidelines that we use to disqualify people at the encounter stage. I call it the "no" list. The longer your "no" list, the fewer men or women you will get to know.

If you take a good look at your "no" list, you'll notice that a lot of your guidelines have nothing to do with what you're looking for in a relationship.

Do you rule out men who are younger or women who are

older? What about men with beards? Gold chains? Birken-
stocks? Women with too much makeup? Maybe you won't
date a man who makes less money than you do. Or a woman
who makes more.

You could probably fill a Dumpster with the rules you
have about how a person should dress, groom, dance, speak,
eat, talk, and walk. Did I leave out accessorize? You should
put these considerations on hold until you get a chance to
check out the things that really matter. You know, the stuff
that you really end up living with, like their convictions and
character. A gold chain can be removed; a bad personality is
here for the duration.

Instead of relying on preconceived notions about what
kind of people are right for you, you should focus on how you
feel about yourself when you're with them. Ask yourself,
"Am I having a good time?" "Does he or she bring out my
good qualities?" "Do I feel respected, listened to, attractive?" "Do I like myself when I'm with him or her?"

My friend Ted complained to me recently about his on-
again, off-again relationship with a gorgeous actress. He told
me they fought a lot and did not want the same things from
the relationship. She was not supportive or respectful of the
things that were important to him. They had broken up and
he wanted to know if I thought he should fight to get her
back.

I asked him one question, "Are you feeling nurtured in
the relationship?" It took very little thought for him to come
up with the answer "no." The only thing that surprised him
was that he had never asked himself that question.

If you're with someone you've put on a pedestal, you need
to pay very close attention to how you feel when you're with
him or her. Strong feelings of infatuation can really cloud

your judgment. Are you spending most of your time trying to make a good impression? Are you pretending to be someone or something so she or he will like you better? Try looking at the situation realistically and asking yourself whether there's any true compatibility. I don't care if it's Cindy Crawford or Denzel Washington; if you're not having a good time, what are you doing there?

step 6 assignments

1. Describe the kind of person you have thought of as "your type." Include physical characteristics, profession, and personality traits.

2. Have a conversation this week with three men/women who are not your type.

3. Get in touch with someone from your past who was interested in you but who you "screened out."

4. Write your "no" list—the criteria you have used to screen people out. Write down every reason you have given for not going out with people in the past: for example, he's bald; she's too short; she has red hair; he doesn't make enough money. Now, pare your list down to only three items that represent core values.

get used to rejection

*

Y ou finally build up the nerve to ask her out and she tells you, sorry, but she's busy Tuesday, and next Friday, and the second Saturday in October. "In fact," she says, "I'm pretty much booked up for the rest of the year."

If you get a queasy feeling in your stomach from reading this, you probably feel the same way about rejection as most people do—you hate it!

People often ask me how to keep from being rejected. I tell them they're already masters at this. Most people have organized their lives around avoiding rejection. They hide out, keep busy, and say they don't have time or interest in a relationship. They use their jobs, children, and any other responsibility they have as an excuse not to put themselves out there.

The bad news is that if you want to find a relationship, you have to get rejected. There's no way around rejection;

you will have to go through it again. And again. And again and again and again. It's just a fact of life.

The good news is that you can learn to deal with rejection more effectively and get through it with a lot less pain than you think.

Let's look at how you've handled rejection in the past. You've tried curling up in a fetal position and downing a quart of Ben and Jerry's. Or whining, pouting, and overanalyzing the situation till even the Psychic Friends Network won't take your calls. Or you've gotten mad and bitterly raised your fist to heaven, solemnly swearing, "As God is my witness, I'll never date again."

Here's a little secret: It isn't you. That's right. This thing that's turned you into a mass of quivering insecurities—it's not personal. Remember in Chapter 6 where we discussed your screening criteria? Until you saw the need to screen people in instead of out, you were rejecting them left and right for the flimsiest of offenses. A beard or lack of one, red hair, a southern accent, the wrong job—any of these were sufficient grounds for disqualification.

Chances are you're being rejected for equally arbitrary reasons. Look, no matter how wonderful you are, some physical characteristic that you do or don't have, what you do for a living, or how you dress is going to be enough to put you on somebody's "no" list. If they're using superficial criteria to screen, they'll dismiss you without a second thought.

When you realize that the reason she didn't smile at you was because of your shoes or that the real reason he's bailing from the conversation is he found out you smoke . . . how can you take it personally?

Once you see how impersonal most rejection is, you won't

spend so much time recovering from it. Most time spent focusing on emotional wounds or analyzing what happened is wasted time. You need to get over rejection as quickly as possible.

Remember, you're going to have to go through a lot of people to get to the one who's right for you. You have high standards, so do other people. And a lot of people simply won't like you. That's okay. I think it's essential to a good relationship that the other person like you.

It's not important to know why someone didn't like you. You just need to get over it and get on to the next person. It is important, however, to know when you're being rejected, and it's not always that obvious. Almost never will someone say, "I don't want to go out with you because I really don't like you." They'll make up an excuse. "It's tax season," or "I have relatives coming in from out of town."

My rule of thumb: If they're not making time for you, consider yourself rejected. This is another time when actions speak louder than words. Clinging to the remote possibility that someone might be available in a few months won't get you any closer to this person who doesn't really like you, and it will postpone your being with someone who does.

A lawyer I know told me a woman he asked out in July said she was in the middle of a big project at work, and suggested he call her back in the fall. I told him that was her way of rejecting him and advised him to ask other women out. His reply: "Why should I date other women when I've already found a woman I'm interested in? Besides, I think she likes me. Why else would she ask me to call her back?"

And this is a bright, college-educated man.

The postscript? Do I have to tell you?

Okay, he called her back after Labor Day and asked her

out again. She said she was still busy, and asked him to call back after Christmas.

I'm telling you, if someone is interested, they'll make time. If Mel Gibson or Demi Moore were in town, they'd file for an extension on their taxes and make the relatives fend for themselves for one night. The point is: If they're not interested, they won't tell you directly. They'll tell you the same way you tell other people—by not making time.

Once you know how to tell when you've been rejected, you need to know how to deal with the pain. Rejection hurts, and pretending it doesn't isn't going to help you achieve your goal.

There is, however, a fine line between feeling the disappointment of a broken heart and wallowing in the pain you feel. People often use the fact that they were rejected to avoid opening up again. They take time off from relationships to analyze what went wrong and to give themselves a chance to heal. Most of their analysis is unproductive. What went wrong is that he or she didn't like you. Don't look for hidden significance. In relationships as in riding, the best thing you can do is to get right back on the horse.

Another mistake people often make is to justify rejection as an attempt to avoid the pain. I can't tell you how often I've heard women say, "I'm powerful and it intimidates men." Or a man say, "I'm too nice, women just like the guys who treat them badly."

A woman I know went to a therapist because she had so much difficulty in her relationships with men. The therapist told her that love couldn't get in or out because her heart was covered over with scar tissue. I thought that was an apt metaphor for describing what happens to people who handle rejection by closing down.

Relationships aren't designed for "playing it safe." When it's safe is when you don't care. The minute you care, it's no longer safe, because you can be hurt, but it's only at that point that it's possible for you to have a meaningful relationship.

You can't wait until you're sure it's going to work out before you open up. You can't say, "I won't get close until I know she or he is right for me," because the only way you're going to discover whether she or he is right for you is by getting close.

I personally had more first dates with no second dates than anyone I've ever met. I must have experienced every possible nuance of rejection there is. It was obvious to me I was doing something wrong. My solution was to change. I'd replace the old Nita with a new, improved, nonrejectable model.

I managed to find a few of the men who had rejected me and quizzed them on the subject. They said I was "loud and pushy."

It seemed pretty obvious men don't like "loud and pushy," so I decided to become demure. I had as much chance of becoming demure as Shaquille O'Neal has of becoming petite. Even if I could have pulled it off, becoming something or someone else wasn't the solution to my problem. What I really needed was to find someone who liked "loud and pushy." Granted, there aren't very many men who do, but fortunately, all I needed was one.

My husband, Tony, is very quiet and reserved. One of his biggest pleasures is watching me in action. At the airport, he'll take our son aside and point to a crowded terminal gate. "See that plane? It's overbooked; they're not letting anyone else on. But watch Mom; we'll be boarding that plane in ten minutes."

A lot of men couldn't stand going out to dinner with me. Tony doesn't care if I send an order back fifteen times. He wouldn't do it, but seeing me do it is a source of amusement for him.

A woman who took my seminar in Phoenix had a unique problem. "I make a lot of money," she said. "My income is in the top five percent of the country. I'm very successful, but I find that men can't handle it. Even men who make a lot of money themselves don't like it when a woman is too successful. What should I do?"

I agreed. A lot of men can't handle being with extremely successful women. But, I reminded her, she was only looking for *one* who could. That night a lot of men came up to her and said they'd like to interview for the part.

You don't have to give up something great about yourself to find a relationship. That's absurd.

At one point during the period I was dating before I met Tony, I was so sick of rejection I just gave up. I said the same things you've probably said: "What am I doing? This is awful. Besides, I have great friends. I don't need a relationship. I'm fine on my own. That's it, I'm not going out anymore." These were good arguments. My roommate was convinced. I even bought them—for a while. But after a couple of days it dawned on me. I thought, "If I quit now, I will probably live the rest of my life without a mate."

So I climbed back on the horse. Within a couple of weeks I met a man I really liked. We went out for several weeks and I thought, "This might be it." Then we spent an incredible weekend skiing together and I was sure he was "the one." The weekend must have been a turning point for him, too. On Sunday our idyllic trip was cut short when he told me that he had decided to go back to his ex-girlfriend.

A single thought rang in my head: *"Quit!"*

That night I was despondent. I knew I needed to go out and meet someone new, but I had really hit rock bottom. I was so depressed I didn't just want to crawl into my bed, I wanted to crawl under it.

Somehow I managed to get myself dressed, made-up, and out of the house. I reminded myself I needed to go someplace where I could meet people, not some quiet restaurant where I could sit in a dark corner and drown my sorrow in a Diet Pepsi. I halfheartedly chose a local bar.

That was the night I met Tony.

Once I met Tony, I could look back on my relationships with other men from a different perspective. I had to go through a lot of people to find him—a *lot*. But in retrospect, I could see that every one of the men who had rejected me had done me a service, because with each rejection from Mr. Wrong I got one step closer to Mr. Right.

If I had quit when it hurt too much, I would have quit one step short of my goal. The temptation to shut down was great. But had I let frustration win, I would have missed out on the love of my life.

By the way, there is one other *very* effective way of handling rejection, but it's not for the fainthearted. If you really like someone and you think he or she has rejected you for the wrong reasons, or wouldn't reject you if he or she got to know you better, reject the rejection!

When people reject you, they expect you to become pitiful and pathetic, to fall apart before their eyes. A confident reaction is the last thing they expect. When you respond by telling them they've made a mistake and that you know they'd really like you if they spent more time with you, it really throws them. Self-esteem is very attractive. They will think twice—and they will probably give you a second chance.

This is exactly what Tony did after I rejected him. Instead of accepting my rejection, he called me back and asked me out again. When I asked him later why he did that, he said he wanted to give me another chance. Tony may be quiet and shy, but he has very high self-esteem. And when he gave me that response, I was impressed.

I can hear you saying, "No way. I could never do that." Fine. Don't. I can't make you do anything, but I can tell you that less than 3 percent of the people in my seminars say they give a good first impression. Odds are you're among the more than 97 percent who don't. So basically, you're being rejected and the person doesn't even know who you are.

If you really like someone and think that once she or he got to know you, she or he would feel differently, why not risk it? What have you got to lose? After all, this is a person who has already rejected you.

step 7 assignment

Validate your progress.

Schedule a meeting (or a phone call) with your support person to review the progress you've made so far toward finding a relationship. Talk about what this project has been like for you, what you've learned, what insights have been most important, and what you are most excited about. Be sure to let your partner know how her or his support has made a difference.

Don't dwell on your fears and doubts, although it's okay to mention them. The purpose of this assignment is to validate your successes.

Don't tell your partner, "It was great that I overcame

my fear and told that guy I found him attractive, but since he never asked me out, I guess it didn't make any difference . . ." Acknowledge even small signs of progress: that you found yourself smiling at people spontaneously; that you told your neighbor you're looking for a relationship; that you went out with a woman who you didn't think was "your type." Every step you take is getting you closer to your goal.

just say no

*

this entire chapter can be summed up in five short words: Don't have sex too soon. This advice is not based on morality or health, neither of which are my field. It is limited to the aspect of sex about which I am an expert: sex as it affects your project of establishing a relationship.

In an earlier chapter, I told you the biggest mistake people make in the area of relationships is that they screen people out too quickly. When they finally screen someone in, they move directly to the second biggest mistake: jumping into bed too quickly. Having sex too soon has kept more potentially good relationships from getting off the ground than any other factor.

You may have already noticed this phenomenon in your own experience. The main reason having sex too soon tends to interfere with a new relationship is because of what I call the "intimacy gap." This is the disparity between the level of emotional intimacy and physical intimacy you are capable of experiencing with someone you've just met. When emotional intimacy is at a two or three on a scale of ten and physical intimacy is at a ten, you're in the intimacy gap.

This gap is characterized by confusion—"Where do I stand?"—and expectation—"When will I see him or her again?" It is the reason for the "morning after" syndrome, the embarrassment and awkwardness people so often feel when they wake up next to someone who is practically a stranger.

When you have sex, it sets up an expectation that this is a relationship. Having this expectation when you have known someone for only a short time is inappropriate. It puts pressure on both of you. At this stage, the bond between you is simply too fragile to withstand this pressure. Instead, it stifles the growth and development that would otherwise naturally occur. The result is often that the relationship gets nipped in the bid.

Because of this pressure, one of you (let's face it, it's usually the man) withdraws—not because he or she doesn't care, is unfeeling, or was using you, but because he or she doesn't know how to deal with the embarrassment and awkwardness and unclarity about expectations.

When sex doesn't cause one of you to bolt, it can propel you into couplehood too soon, which can give rise to the "buyer's remorse" syndrome. Karen is a good example of this. When I met her, Karen, a professional in her thirties who lives in L.A., was dating a guy named Kent. They had immediate chemistry, she told me, and had sex on their third date. Now, a month later, they were "a couple," and she was beginning to realize he wasn't right for her. She said, "I wish I hadn't slept with him, because it would be so much easier to break it off."

When you're attracted to someone right away, that attraction is often based on initial chemistry. As we discussed in the step 6 chapter, initial chemistry is untrustworthy as an indicator of relationship potential. If there's nothing behind the chemistry, it's better to find that out before you have sex.

I recommend that you wait until after you've had at least eight dates with someone before you have sex. The main purpose for the Nita Tucker Eight-Date Rule is to support you in taking the time to develop a relationship before you have sex with someone. (By the way, if you just want to get laid, go ahead. You can do it in the first fifteen minutes—what do I care. The eight-date rule applies when you think there is a possibility for more than a one-night stand or a fling.)

People in my seminars whine and argue more about the eight-date rule than about any other piece of advice. Someone always asks, "What about my friends who slept together on their first date and have been happily married for years?"

Those friends are just like the couples who met when neither of them were looking for relationships, or the ones who are happily married to their "type." Of course it happens. It's just that the chances of it happening to you are extremely slim. Once again, it's a question of odds. Remember, we want them on your side.

A lot of people have the mistaken idea that if they go out with someone two or three times, it means they're in a relationship. To expect that you're in a relationship with someone you've seen only a few times is inappropriate. This is someone you're just getting to know. You may be infatuated and feel like you've known each other forever, but trust me, you haven't.

This was brought home to me again recently when I got together with my friend Sharon for coffee. She told me about

a man she had met a few weeks before. "You don't understand, Nita," she told me. "We stayed up all night talking.
We told each other things we've never told anyone else. We're
so much alike, it's like we're the same person—we even both
have older brothers who live in the Midwest. And I don't
know why I haven't heard from him."

So what do you do when it's your third or fourth date and
you really like this person. It's late at night and things are
hot and heavy. You are excited and turned on. You're really
horny. You can't stand the frustration. What do you do? You
do the same thing you tell your kids to do. You wait. You
take a cold shower.

I'm all for passion, for being spontaneous, and for being
in touch with your emotions. Your emotions are wonderful;
just don't put them in charge of this decision. If you do,
you'll end up going to bed every time.

Don't wait until you're locked in an embrace to say, "I'd
really love to make love with you but I read this book. I forgot
her name, but the author has this eight-date rule." If this is
my rule and not your rule, it's not going to work. You've got
to think this through and make a decision—ahead of time.
By resolving in advance that you are going to act in your own
best interests, you will be better equipped to exercise self-
discipline when the time comes.

Learn how to say no. Say, "I'd love to make love to you.
I'm attracted to you. I'm turned on by you. I just want to
wait until we know each other better."

People have told me, "I'm a grown-up. I can't just neck
in the car." If you're a grown-up, stop being so self-indulgent.
Stop going for instant gratification. Be mature enough to
make constructive choices that are consistent with what you
really want in life.

Besides, when was the last time you went to bed at night feeling excited, turned on, and frustrated? When was the last time you were kept awake tossing and turning with anticipation? Enjoy it while it lasts. Going to bed frustrated is preferable to waking up feeling empty and disappointed.

A note for men: A lot of men have told me they're afraid women will think they're wimps if they don't come on to them. They've been trained to think they have to beg for sex from the first date on through thirty years of marriage. What they haven't learned is that saying no can be the best way to get someone to want you. I'm not advising you to be asexual or platonic. Quite the opposite. Following the eight-date rule should not prevent you from coming across as virile and sexy. When you make it clear that a relationship is more important to you than an orgasm, don't be surprised if you find naked women in your bed.

When I was giving my seminar in Dallas, a guy named Chris came up to me during the break, right after I talked about this. He told me how right I was. He said that because of his religious convictions he was not going to have sex outside of marriage. "I had to change the locks on my door three times," he told me.

This rule applies to gay people as well. Brian was a gay man who took my seminar in Seattle. He told me, "Nita, you don't understand gay culture. Men don't wait to have sex with each other." After we reviewed the last eight months of his dating history, it became painfully obvious to him that his embrace of "gay culture" had resulted in a number of one-night stands, a few three- or four-night stands, and a lot of loneliness and disappointment. I ran into him a couple of years later at a party. He introduced me to the man he was living with, then took me aside to tell me that the eight-date rule was the turning point for him.

Remember, the rule is that you don't have sex any sooner than the eighth date, not that you have to have sex as soon as you hit the eighth date. What many people find when they get to that point is that they still don't feel they're in a relationship yet or that they're not ready to stop seeing other people. If you have the slightest question in your mind about whether he or she is going to call or see you after you go to bed with him or her, it's too soon. If you aren't sure whether you're ready, err on the side of waiting too long.

By the way, only one date a day counts. If you had breakfast together, then lunch, then cocktails, then went to a movie, you did not have four dates—you had one long one. (Nice try, though.)

sex *does not equal* love

Sandra is a thirty-one-year-old woman who owns her own clothing company. Before she took my seminar, she would jump into bed with guys as soon as she felt there was potential for a relationship. More than sex itself, she liked the intimacy she felt when she cuddled with her lover afterward.

For Sandra, sex was a way of feeling closer to a man. Like many women, she tried to use it as a shortcut to love. But while sex can be an expression of love, it is not a means of achieving it any more than eating at expensive restaurants is a means of achieving wealth.

A lot of people, like Sandra, view sex as a way of experiencing love and bonding. This tends to be truer for women, who are much more likely to equate sex with intimacy and affection than men. Having sex because you want closeness, cuddling, and real bonding is an approach that usually back-fires. It's true that sex can induce these feelings, but it does so in much the same way that a drug can bring about feelings of euphoria. The drug high wears off as soon as the physical stimulus that gave rise to it is gone. The same thing happens with the intimacy high. And after you crash, you're left feeling more lonely and isolated than before.

Intimacy, love, and affection have to be earned. There is no shortcut to these feelings. Unless they are based on shared experiences and mutual understanding and appreciation, they do not have a foundation. They're like a mirage that disappears when you get closer.

You have to ask yourself what having sex means to you. If it means something, don't do it until that something is there. Don't have sex to get it there.

being single *in the age of* AIDS

Even though health isn't my field, I can't keep my mouth shut about the insanity of having unprotected sex. I am continually shocked at how many single people don't take the threat of AIDS seriously. These are smart, mature, aware people, but they are in denial about this very serious issue. They think it's okay to have unprotected sex because somehow the threat of AIDS doesn't apply to them. One man even tried to convince me he could tell that someone he was dating was not infected by the way she looked.

My friend Eric explained to me why he has unprotected sex. He says if sex is a ten without a condom, using a condom makes it a three. The only thing I can say is that sex is a zero if you're dead.

I recommend that before you have unprotected sex you

get tested together. Then, continue to use a condom for least
six months until you get tested again. One couple I know
apparently thought of the test as foreplay—they went back
home right away and had sex to celebrate having taken this
step. According to the latest medical evidence, a waiting
period between tests is necessary to establish with certainty
that you are not infected (consult your physician to determine how long you need to wait).

People have told me they don't feel comfortable asking
someone to get tested. If you're not intimate enough to be
talking about an AIDS test, you're definitely not intimate
enough to have sex.

adjust your attitude

*

finally, you've met the perfect person. You have the relationship you've always wanted and everything is picture-perfect. For a while. Soon, the first cracks begin to appear in the veneer. He makes too much noise when he eats. She has an irritating laugh. He's stingy. She's bossy. You start to fret. You get resentful. You start looking for the exit signs.

Don't panic. The relationship isn't falling apart and you haven't hooked up with the wrong person. It's just your collection of bad attitudes.

From the time you were a small child, you've been collecting tidbits of information on male/female relationships. You observed your family, relatives, and neighbors and used them as role models. But because most of them weren't exactly doing a terrific job at relating, you collected a lot of bad attitudes.

When you enter a new relationship, you bring these negative attitudes, opinions, and fears with you. Eventually, they dictate what your relationships will be like. There's the "men are babies" mantra you borrowed from your aunt Viola. Or your dad's macho adage, "Real men don't even know where the kitchen is." You might have come up with one of your own: "Relationships are a fifty-fifty proposition—you give fifty percent and they take the other fifty."

You don't just keep these outdated, counterproductive opinions in the background. You take on the role of lawyer and use them to build a case. You collect every piece of evidence you can to make a convincing argument that your opinion is actually the truth. If the woman you're dating tells you she'd like to spend some time apart, it could mean she'd enjoy doing some things on her own or it could mean she's sick of being with you. You opt for the latter, because you're building your case that "women always leave." And your paranoia and need for constant reassurance make it more likely that she will leave.

Marriage can be heaven; it can also be hell. Most marriages fall somewhere in the middle with love, support, and generosity mixed with occasional criticism, resentment, and nagging.

If you were exposed to an abusive relationship or one in which the latter qualities were the norm, you probably developed a bad attitude toward the whole institution. But you didn't have to grow up on the set of *Who's Afraid of Virginia Woolf* to end up with negative attitudes concerning relationships. Even in a happy home, there is ample opportunity for an impressionable child to learn about the darker side of male/female bonding.

Most likely your parents had a fight or two in front of you. That was all it took for you to decide relationships are full of struggle. If your mother had to account to your father for the money she spent, you might have concluded that, in marriage, women answer to men or women don't know how to handle money. And if one of your parents asked you to conceal something from the other, you got the idea that deception is a normal part of relationships.

Witnessing violence or excessive criticism or being told of sexual indiscretions or inadequacies gives most children the impression that "marriage is painful," and, tragically for many, it results in a fear of closeness and intimacy.

Your parents didn't strive to be bad role models. They were, for the most part, doing the best they could. Most of them mated for those functional reasons we discussed earlier. Women often stayed in unsatisfying marriages because separation or divorce meant financial insecurity. And a lot of men toughed out unhappy unions to avoid the taboo of divorce and its effect on their standing in the community.

Many of the bad attitudes you formed came from observing their sadness and frustration and their feelings of being trapped. Even those of you whose families were happy ones collected your share of unconstructive notions about relationships.

It wasn't just what your parents said or did that influenced you. You soaked up every cultural, generational, and personal point of view they held about men and women. And when you grew up and noticed that the world had changed, did you go back and revise these views? No, you didn't even question whether they were still applicable. You just plopped them down in the middle of each relationship, then wondered why it didn't last.

Later, your own relationships became the source of negative attitudes. You'd experience frustration, anger, jealousy, and loss and rack up dozens of new negative opinions. If you went through a divorce, you added scores to your already extensive collection of pessimistic views. And with a lingering sense of disillusionment and failure came decisions like, "I'll never get involved with another divorced woman," or "I don't want a man who is married to his career." And, even more damaging, you vowed to never be that vulnerable again.

You don't live in the restricted world of your parents and grandparents. You have choices and options. But to the extent that your attitudes are dictating your behavior, they are limiting the choices you can make. If your behavior is controlled by the negative attitudes and decisions you've made, you're reacting instead of making choices. To make choices, you have to release the hold these attitudes have had on you.

Exposing your negative attitudes is the first step you can take toward being able to have the kind of relationship you really want. The next step is to become aware of how these attitudes have been holding you back.

Nora, a successful travel consultant, had a full life with lots of friends and outside interests. She did not want to get married. She avoided relationships with men, feeling she was better off without them. What, then, was she doing in my seminar? Her mother bribed her!

We got to the part of the course where we examine the attitudes we hold about relationships and I did a bit of probing. Nora talked about her mother, whose life she considered to be boring and uneventful. She had always felt disappointed that her mother had sacrificed so many of her dreams for the sake of the family. She had come to equate relationships with "selling out" and had chosen her single lifestyle to avoid a similar loss of identity.

She discovered that her belief that relationships stifled women came from a negative attitude she had formed in childhood, and saw that getting married didn't mean she'd have to give up everything she'd worked for to lead a life of sacrifice and boredom. She saw that her "choice" to live alone had been dictated by her reaction to her mother's experiences.

Being alone is definitely preferable to being in a bad relationship. But for the vast majority of people, being in a loving, supportive relationship is far better than being alone. If your negative attitudes are strong enough, they will cause you to give up on relationships altogether.

Nick took my seminar hoping it would help him find a relationship, but he was hardly enthusiastic. When we exposed his list of negative attitudes, he saw that he had accepted a belief that a committed relationship would mean the fun would stop. He assumed if he got involved he could no longer go out with the boys, spend money, go fishing, or even stay late at work.

Nick's negative opinions didn't keep him out of relationships the way Nora's did, but they created an ambivalence that was at odds with his deeper desire to be involved with someone.

Shelley, a new widow, had been married for thirteen years. Her marriage had been marked by friction, competitiveness, and one-upsmanship—just like the marriages she observed in her self-described family of ogres and nut cases.

Shelley's bad attitudes made her repeat history rather than learn from it. She assumed that the kind of destructive relationships she had grown up with were inevitable. And she personally had so much evidence to prove this point, she had trouble seeing the possibility that relationships could ever be any other way.

Many people find that their partnerships are replicas of

the less-than-perfect relationships they observed as children. These childhood impressions can be so deeply rooted that it doesn't occur to people to try to break out of them. They just can't imagine that their relationships could be better. They simply resign themselves to the limitations of unfulfilling partnerships and say, "It's the way marriage is."

Sometimes our unconscious attitudes and fears come in the form of "sabotage patterns"—the particular ways that we go about destroying our relationships. I was shocked to discover my own sabotage pattern one night when Tony and I were having dinner with my girlfriend Leslie. I had been dating Tony for about a month and I was excited to show him off.

"Tony," I said, "tell Leslie how you got your job with the Sonics." He did, and when he finished, I filled in the parts he had left out.

A few minutes later I said, "Tony, tell Leslie that funny story you told me last night." Again he told her, and again I embellished his story with details I thought made it more amusing and more to the point.

Before long, Leslie and I were doing all the talking. Tony played with objects on the table—his spoon, his water glass, his napkin, my fingers.

By the time we finished dinner I was embarrassed, angry, and upset. I thought Tony was acting like a jerk. I decided then and there that I would not continue to see him. I couldn't have a relationship with a man who acted like a child.

As we walked across the parking lot to the car, it hit me—a realization so powerful that I will never forget it.

I realized that Tony had become progressively less interested in talking as the evening wore on. What I saw as "childish" behavior was his way of reacting to my repeated interruptions and corrections. I guess he figured it was inefficient for both of us to have to say what was on his mind. Talk about acting like a jerk!

I couldn't stand seeing that I'd suppressed him in that way. But that wasn't the end of my realization. In a flash I saw that I had similarly suppressed every man I'd ever been with. I hadn't done it on purpose or even consciously; I had done it in such a subtle way that not only had I not seen it, no one else had seen it either. But I saw it now, and the truth was inescapable: I had destroyed every relationship I'd had by inhibiting and dominating the men I had gone out with.

I didn't think of it as suppression at the time. I thought I was "helping them improve," or "offering useful advice." In fact, most men I dated told me I was the most perceptive woman they'd ever met. But my insights always pointed out their flaws and inadequacies. And after a steady diet of these "insights," they would inevitably lose confidence in themselves.

My explanation for this phenomenon always cast the blame on the man. "He couldn't stand up to a powerful woman," or "He couldn't handle me because I'm too smart." But in that moment in the parking lot I saw that I had spent my life looking for a man who would not become dependent, yet had always found a way to bring men's weaknesses to the forefront.

For a moment, I hated myself, but then the third part of the realization hit.

I saw that my ability to turn men into wimps and bring out their weakness could be turned around. That I could use the same power to help bring out the best in them. I saw that now I would finally be able to have a successful relationship.

This realization was a major turning point for me. Once I saw how I had been sabotaging my relationships, I could see how to stop doing it.

Everyone I have ever worked with has sabotaged their relationships to one degree or another. None of them saw it, however, until they looked for it. And in every case, discovering how they did it was the first step toward turning it around. And in the course of doing this, they discovered that they—not their mates, their circumstances, or luck—were responsible for how their relationships turned out.

The first thing to know about your pattern of sabotage is that it's hidden. That's pretty obvious, right? If you knew what you were doing to destroy your relationships, you'd stop doing it. But your method of sabotage is not just hidden, it's cleverly disguised as "what men always do," or "what keeps going wrong."

Although the fact that you're the one responsible for destroying your relationships may sound like bad news, it's really good news. If you're the one destroying them, you're the one who can stop destroying them.

It's very difficult for some people to accept that they are responsible for the way their relationships turn out, because when they see what they've been doing, they feel like jerks. Realizing that I had suppressed men and destroyed all my past relationships did not make me feel proud of myself, but it was the key to my being able to start behaving differently in new relationships.

We've already seen that one reason you destroy relationships is because of your fears and negative attitudes. Undoubtedly, there are many other reasons at the root of why people undermine their relationships, but fortunately, it isn't necessary for you to analyze these in order to stop doing it.

Who cares why you've been screwing it up as long as you stop? Finding out how you sabotage will help enable you to stop.

In the following pages I identify eight pattern "stereotypes." One or more of them may apply to your situation. Each pattern is broken down into three parts: "How you see it," "What's really going on," and "What to do about it." See if you recognize yourself in any of them.

PATTERN 1

* *how you see it.* Liking the chase.

Are you always attracted to the people you can't have, the "hard to get" ones? Do you lose interest in someone once he or she falls for you? Are you easily bored? Do you hate it when they "fall all over you?"

There are several variations to the "liking the chase" pattern: going after the most popular or unattainable guy, but when you "get" him, feeling as if you won the booby prize; a string of relationships that fall apart because you always lose interest in the woman after a while; liking people who treat you with indifference, but when they act nice to you it feels as if they're clinging.

* *what's really going on.* This pattern has nothing to do with liking a challenge. It is all about low self-esteem—yours. Groucho Marx used to joke, "I wouldn't want to belong to any club that would accept me as a member." If you have this pattern, you wouldn't want to be in a relationship with anyone who has poor enough taste to be in love with someone like you.

But if you can't love someone who loves you, you're not going to be able to have much of a relationship.

✳ *what to do about it.* Next time a partner starts being appreciative and attentive, don't run away screaming and don't pronounce him or her a bore. Instead, see if you can bring yourself to endure this intolerable experience. Give yourself a chance to see how it feels to be liked. Notice how much you want to run away, but instead of doing it, remind yourself that liking you is a sign of someone's good taste!

PATTERN 2

✳ *how you see it.* I give more than I get.

Do others take advantage of you? Are you always the one who "gives" in a relationship? Do you think most men/women are "takers"? You're always there with patience, understanding, and kindness when they need you, but they don't treat you the same way.

✳ *what's really going on.* Doormats say "welcome" on them, and every martyr has a persecutor. If you have this pattern, you're not happy unless you're mistreated, so you manipulate others into doing just that.

To keep your partners from being as good as you are, you ask them to do things for you when you know they have no time. Or you ask in such an accusatory way that they have to say no. When they do try to do things for you, you don't react graciously—you complain that whatever they did wasn't done right.

True giving is free and is done for the giver's pleasure. If you're keeping score, it's not giving.

✳ *what to do about it.* It's important for you to keep a close watch on your actions in order to resist your tendency to "give" as a means of manipulating. When you do give, don't keep score. Stop looking at what he or she is doing or not doing for you, and when someone does something nice, even something small, be appreciative.

PATTERN 3

✳ *how you see it*. Others leave me for no reason.

Are you always surprised when a relationship ends? Did you think it was going really well? You know you never do anything that drives them away—you never nag or expect too much. And you're always careful to avoid conflict.

✳ *what's really going on*. People with this pattern have their heads buried in the sand. Barry was the classic ostrich. The last girlfriend he had before he took my seminar left him suddenly, just like the others. For him, her departure "came out of the blue." He speculated that she left him because she was going through a midlife crisis.

What he realized in my seminar was that by avoiding conflict, he had not addressed any of the problems that existed in the relationship. He thought if he ignored them they would go away, but of course they didn't.

With his unwillingness to communicate about anything uncomfortable, there wasn't much to talk about. So much was avoided, there was nothing left to share. His "don't rock the boat" attitude made his relationships boring and mundane.

✳ *what to do about it*. Start noticing when you want to ignore the issues that arise in your relationships. Stop letting them go by. When your discomfort threatens to keep you from communicating, remind yourself what refusing to confront issues costs you.

Remember that your commitment to making the relationship successful is more powerful than your fears. Enlist the help of your support partner; tell her or him to insist that you communicate about whatever is going on.

PATTERN 4

✳ *how you see it.* Others are threatened by your power.

Do people tell you how insightful you are? Do you feel your strength is overpowering? Are you supportive? Always offering helpful advice? Do you tend to become their "adviser?"

✳ *what's really going on.* This, as you may recall, was my pattern. I tried to "help" men by pointing out how they could improve and by constantly correcting them. If you have this pattern, you probably consider yourself to be very perceptive. You think you're using your insight to help the people you date, but what you're actually doing is constantly finding and pointing out their faults. The message they get from you, however subtle, is that they're not okay.

The people you date did much better before they got involved with you. Once they start dating you, they become dependent. They stop making decisions because they know you'll only reverse them. They become addicted to your advice. As their self-confidence diminishes, they become less and less attractive to you.

✳ *what to do about it.* Start using your intelligence and perceptiveness to build people up instead of down. For example, she asks you, "What do you think?" Instead of giving your usually brilliant answer, ask her what she thinks. When she tells you, don't disagree and don't offer a better solution. You may at first have trouble trusting her answers, because you're so used to your way being the best way. Don't be surprised, however, if the solutions she comes up with are better than yours. Learn to trust her decisions—after all, it was her competence and self-assurance that attracted you to her in the first place.

PATTERN 5

✳ *how you see it*. I become a wimp when I'm involved with someone I care about.

Does all the ease and confidence you feel in your professional life fly out the window the minute you're around someone you really like? Do you avoid saying what's on your mind because you're worried you'll look pushy? When you get involved in a relationship, do you get needy and clingy? Do you become intensely focused on the relationship?

✳ *what's really going on*. You are dependent on others for your identity. You're "nobody till somebody loves you." You can probably point to your long list of accomplishments and professional successes to prove how independent you are, but underneath you feel you need a mate.

If you're like most people who have this pattern, you seem anything but dependent. In fact, it is your fear of dependency that motivates you to put so much energy into your career. Your achievements are a way of compensating for the desperation you feel about being without a relationship.

The career you've established is worthwhile, in and of itself. But rather than solving your basic problem, it only covers it up. Basing your identity on your work and accomplishments isn't going to fill the void you feel without a mate.

✳ *what to do about it*. You're so used to covering up your feelings of desperation about needing someone that just admitting you feel this way is a great step forward. Next time you notice the desperate or clingy feelings coming over you, see if you can observe them instead of trying to cover them up.

Don't stop achieving things, but do stop looking to your accomplishments to provide you with a sense of identity and worth. Instead, you need to discover that your worthwhile qualities are not dependent on your outward achievements.

PATTERN 6

✴ *how you see it.* I always fall in love with people who don't return my love.

Do you fall for men or women you can't have? Do you put people on pedestals? Get obsessed? Do you have romantic fantasies about what it would be like if only he or she loved you back? Do you think once you find True Love, your life will be glorious?

✴ *what's really going on.* You aren't in love with a person; you're in love with your image of one. You look at your fantasy lover from afar and see Superman. You think you want him to love you back, but if he did you would get close enough to discover he's only Clark Kent. It would destroy the fantasy and the relationship because your relationship is with the fantasy.

In lieu of a real connection between you and your dream, you are addicted to "hope." You keep this hope alive by fantasizing. Your fear of rejection is at the root of this pattern. The fact that your fantasy lover doesn't return your affection isn't a real rejection, because you think if he really knew you, he would love you.

You may complain that unrequited love is painful, but it's a romantic pain. It's much loftier than the pain that occurs when you deal with the problems of a real relationship. It's easier to keep unrequited love passionate than it is to keep the excitement alive with a real person whose flaws aren't adorable like those of your fantasy. Yours is the easiest kind of relationship to have: one that's never mundane and has no conflicts.

＊*what to do about it.* Next time you find yourself falling into an unrequited love affair, ask yourself if you would rather have a fantasy relationship or a real one. Then face reality: If the person you're crazy about isn't asking you out, he probably isn't interested. If he isn't interested now, he's not going to suddenly get interested. Your hope that he will is not based on reality.

You need to stop dwelling on these "dream" people. Resist the impulse to fantasize about them and don't feed your tendency to get obsessed with them by keeping things around that make you think of them or going to places where you may run into them.

This pattern isn't just about worshiping from afar. If you find yourself in on-line or long-distance relationships that are rarely face-to-face, odds are this is your pattern.

PATTERN 7

＊*how you see it.* I get involved with men/women who can't be trusted.

Have you been burned one too many times? Lied to? Cheated on? Have you made up your mind that you're not going to let someone get close to you again unless you're sure he or she won't violate your trust?

＊*what's really going on.* Yes, you've been hurt, and yes, by protecting yourself you won't get hurt again. But you also won't have a relationship. The protective fortress you've erected around yourself is keeping Mr. or Ms. Right out along with the people who might hurt you. The requirement that someone prove his or her trustworthiness before you'll allow yourself to get close keeps you unavailable for relationships.

✻ *what to do about it.* You have to be willing to risk getting hurt. In order for you to fall in love, your heart has to be open enough that it could be broken. Getting to know someone and letting someone get to know you is the only way to find out if you're right for each other.

PATTERN 8

✻ *how you see it.* I always fall for the wrong person.

Do you always get involved with someone who isn't good for you? Do you wonder why you keep picking people who aren't right for you and then ask yourself why you stick with them?

These symptoms could describe any of three different patterns.

✻ *scenario one: what's really going on.* "I always pick the wrong person" is an excuse you use to avoid taking responsibility.

The man who becomes a wimp when he's with an "undermining" woman could be powerful and self-assured when he's with someone more supportive. A man who is unwilling to commit to a "desperate" woman might turn around and commit to someone whose neediness is not driving him away. The same woman who takes advantage of a "manipulator" might become an angel with a man who isn't forcing her into the role of "taker."

If the "wrong ones" you've been picking seem to improve when they get involved with someone else, your problem isn't that you pick the wrong ones, it's that you turn them into the wrong ones.

❋ *scenario one: what to do about it.* Reread Patterns 1–7 to discover your actual sabotage pattern.

❋ *scenario two: what's really going on.* You think love is scarce, that there is only one man or woman or very few whom you could possibly love, so you consider love an overriding reason to stay with someone. You think you should stick it out with someone you love even if he or she doesn't treat you well, even if the relationship is terrible.

Love is one ingredient that is required for a successful partnership between a man and a woman. It is by no means the only necessary ingredient, and it does not "conquer all." It is not a good reason to stay with someone who isn't right for you.

❋ *scenario two: what to do about it.* Realize that love is not scarce. This man or woman isn't the only one you could love. You could also love someone who treats you well, so don't sell yourself short.

❋ *scenario three: what's really going on.* If you keep ending up with people who are abusive or violent, who are alcoholics or substance abusers, or whose behavior is self-destructive or destructive to those around them, you really are picking "the wrong ones."

❋ *scenario three: what to do about it.* If this is the case, you may want to seek support from someone who is trained in helping people overcome this type of problem.

now *what?*

You may have clearly recognized your pattern among those described. You may even see yourself in several of them. You may have some but not all of the symptoms of a particular pattern. You may have found a pattern that has shown up in some but not all of your relationships.

For every pattern there is a range from severe to mild. One man with an unrequited love pattern may become obsessed with a woman he has never even met. Another might get involved with women who love him back but less intensely than he loves them. Same pattern, different degrees.

Remember, these are pattern stereotypes, and stereotypes are never exactly like real life. If the description of a pattern doesn't fit you like a glove, don't quibble. If it has any elements that apply to your situation, you will benefit from taking the position that it is a form of sabotage you are practicing.

Maybe you don't see your pattern clearly or understand how you're actually sabotaging relationships. Assuming responsibility when you can't see clearly how you are sabotaging might require a leap of faith. But once you're willing to see yourself as the saboteur, the insight as to how you do it will dawn on you. There's one thing you can't miss: You're the common link. You're the only one who was there each time a relationship failed.

What if you think you have no pattern? This may seem like a laudable position to be in, but it's not. Unless you can discover how you undermine your relationships, you will not be able to stop doing it. If the problems in your relationships are not caused by you, you cannot correct them.

It's in your own best interest to discover how you sabotage relationships, so I suggest you go back to the beginning of this chapter and review the material. Then reread the descriptions of Patterns 1 through 8, and see if you can find yours. If you only have part of a pattern, or it makes you feel uncomfortable just reading about one, odds are it's yours.

What if you see yourself in every pattern? Don't get nervous, you're not a hopeless case, just a bit overly analytical. Focus on reforming the pattern that gives you the most trouble.

Now that you've identified your pattern, you can begin to turn it around. But don't expect to see your pattern disappear overnight. This behavior is a habit by now, so you will have to exercise discipline in order to stop repeating it.

Before I identified my pattern, I was unaware of my suppressive behavior toward men. Once I knew what to look for, I could catch myself every time I started to behave this way, and stop myself. It took discipline at first, but soon the habit diminished in strength.

As many people with smoking or drinking habits know, tendencies toward a particular behavior pattern may never entirely disappear. You may always need to be aware of your pattern so that you don't fall into it again.

Relationships are rarely easy. If you want one, you're going to have to be willing to fight a lot of battles. And many of those battles, like this one, are going to be with yourself.

step 9 assignments

1. Answer the following questions:

✳ What problems or complaints have you had in your past relationships? What hasn't worked?

✳ What has worked in your past or present relationships? (Think about your most satisfying relationships and list the qualities that were present.)

✳ What do you think you would have to give up if you were married or in a relationship? (For example: freedom; closet space; control over your time or money.)

✳ The trouble with men/women is: (For example: men are babies; women are after one thing; men are after one thing; men are insensitive; women are too sensitive.)

2. Interview two happily married couples about their relationships: Ask about how they met, their first impressions of each other, the ingredients that make their relationships successful, and whether either had a fear of commitment and, if so, how they resolved it.

3. Relationship collage: You'll need poster board, glue, scissors, and a pile of magazines. Go through the magazines and cut out images and words that illustrate what you want in a relationship (you may want to refer back to the "ideal relationship" essay you wrote in the step 2 chapter). Make a collage out of these images and any other items— photographs, drawings, meaningful objects—you would like to include.

People sometimes say they think this exercise sounds silly. It's not. It helps you get in touch with your vision of what a relationship can be and makes your ideal seem less vague and more tangible and attainable. Many of the same people who resisted doing this exercise reported afterward that they found it moving and inspiring.

too familiar story probably depends on whether you are a man or a woman.

Either way, the issue of commitment is one you're going to have to resolve if you want to have a lifetime partnership. In this chapter, I will tell you how.

I have to warn you that what I'm about to say may sound sexist. I'm sorry, but that's the way it is. When one of you is pushing for commitment and the other is backing away from it, it's a great deal more likely that the former is the woman and the latter the man. Yes, it can happen the other way around. But rather than pussyfooting around this, I'm going to talk about it in the terms that are most applicable to the vast majority of couples. If you're a man who wants to commit or a woman who doesn't, please forgive me for stereotyping. Just bear with me and reverse the "she" and "he" in what you're about to read.

The difference between how men and women approach commitment are significant enough that they each have their own definition for the word: (1) a pledge or promise to do something and (2) official consignment . . . of a person to prison, to a mental hospital, etc.

For most women, the first is the preferred definition. Survival of the species may no longer depend on men doing the hunting to provide food and shelter for the family, but millennia of biological conditioning have left women with a natural impulse toward wanting a secure partnership.

For men, the word "commitment" has a more unpleasant connotation. It's about confinement. It's what happens when those guys in the little white coats come to take you away.

This basic male aversion to commitment becomes magnified when the idea of settling down becomes associated, as it is for many men today, with failure.

men *and* commitment: *avoiding failure*

In our culture, manhood is measured by success. Most men are brought up with the notion that to be a man you have to prove yourself and be successful. For most men, there is nothing worse than failing. (Women don't like failure either, but it is not as central to their sense of identity. Being considered unattractive is the female counterpart.)

When a man has a failed relationship or two under his belt, he begins to get wary. As a result, he may be gun-shy about committed relationships and not have a clue that this is really about a fear of repeating failure. On a conscious level, he may want a relationship and even ardently pursue one. When he talks about the family life he values, he means it. But when things develop to the point where a commitment is in the offing, something happens. As soon as it looks as if "this is it," he freaks out and doesn't know why.

What is happening is that he is reminded of the last time things got this close. Warning bells go off. "I can't have a failure," he thinks. "I can't be a two-time (or three-time) loser." The problem is this thought process is unconscious.

This results in the phenomenon of the man who goes gangbusters toward a relationship, then suddenly withdraws.

I get phone call after phone call from women who tell me, "He was the one who pursued the relationship. He was the one who wanted to get serious. He was the one who wanted to move in. And now he's backing out."

I experienced this phenomenon myself when I was dating my husband. After we had been going together for several

months, he asked me to move in with him. I wasn't so sure
I wanted to. I didn't care for his suburban Seattle neighbor-
hood, preferring my place in the city. But I went along with
the move because of his insistence and because I loved him.

My first clue that things weren't going well was that
when I was unpacking, Tony, who is normally very helpful,
was nowhere to be seen. When I looked for him, I found him
sitting alone in the dark. I asked him what was going on. He
gave me the classic male answer: "Nothing."

Suddenly, I sensed what was happening. I asked him if
he was feeling trapped. "Yes," he replied, as if in a trance.

My first reaction was to kill him. This wasn't even my
idea. I wasn't even moving into a place I liked—and he's
accusing me of trapping him! Justification for homicide.

Fortunately, it dawned on me that the divorce he had
been through shortly before I met him was behind all of this.
I thought, now he's setting up housekeeping again; it must
be pretty scary. We started talking about what he was going
through. I suggested that maybe it was too soon for us to be
doing this and offered to move back to my apartment. He
said, "No, I want you to be here. This was my idea."

We went out for dinner and had a very romantic evening.
Things went great—for about a week.

Then one night we were sitting in the living room, talking. I mentioned the idea of our taking a vacation together
that summer. All of a sudden I noticed his eyes begin to glaze
over. He looked upset and became withdrawn. I could practically see the word "trapped" appear across his face. It was
obvious to me but invisible to him.

During the next few months, whenever we talked about
the future, planning a vacation, holidays, anything that made
this seem like a permanent relationship, I would see the same

signs. Each time I noticed the signs, I would ask, "Are you feeling trapped right now?" He would say, "Yes, I am," and I would say, "Oh."

Each time the signs surfaced, I tried to help Tony understand what he was going through by asking him questions like these. I had to keep reminding myself to have compassion, to try to look at what was going on from his point of view. I had to remember each time not to take it personally and not to be hurt by it. This was his process, not mine. I didn't ignore his fear, but neither did I get angry or defensive, or try to change the way he felt. I just understood what he was going through and that he was entitled to these feelings. After four or five months, he got through it.

All too often, women take it personally when a man begins to withdraw. When he begins pulling back, her interpretation is that he doesn't love her as much as he used to. She gets hurt. And this only exacerbates the situation because most men, like most women, hate hurting another person. The woman's hurt feelings can cause the man to pull even farther away because of the guilt he feels in response. This generates a vicious cycle. Often, the outcome is that the man bolts—not because he doesn't care about the woman but because he does. He is trying to escape from the pressure and guilt he feels over hurting someone he cares about.

A huge percentage of single men over thirty are divorced. If they aren't divorced, their parents, or their best friends, or their next door neighbors, or both their sisters are. The divorce rate now is over 55 percent; it's an epidemic. *Newsweek* called it a plague. So, divorce is looming over all single men even if they haven't gone through it themselves.

I don't care what the circumstances were, a divorce is a failure. People don't go down the aisle and say, "If everything goes as planned, in about ten years we should be filing for separation." No matter how much a man might justify a divorce—"I'm much happier now," "It was best for the kids," "We left on good terms," "We still like each other, we just weren't right for each other"—deep down it is still registered as a failure.

Woman often complain about having to put up with male "baggage." I don't know when baggage became such an awful thing. I call it experience. You're dealing with someone who has been molded by the experiences of a full life. If you want someone without baggage, date ten-year-olds.

I tell men they should try to be conscious about what they're going through and to understand it's about fear of failure, not fear of commitment. Men have now been told by so many women that they're afraid to commit, they've started to believe it. I can't tell you how many men have told me they're "a man who can't commit." They're reading books about their "commitment phobia" and going on weekend drumming workshops in the woods with their men's groups to try to get over it. There's nothing wrong with that; it's just that they're treating the wrong disease.

Many men have become so risk-aversive, they aren't even asking women out. They're looking for a surefire, 100 percent guaranteed, lasts forever, no-risk relationship. They think finding the "perfect person" will eliminate the risk. But there is no such thing as a perfect person or a guaranteed relationship.

women *and* commitment: *deadly force*

An even bigger mistake than taking a man's withdrawal personally is trying to force him to commit. Commitment is something that evolves naturally as two people get to know each other, become intimate, and fall in love. Where many women go wrong is they try to hurry this natural process along. Instead of appreciating the companionship, support, and intimacy that are already there, they try to put the relationship into a box, to pin it down.

After they've been with a man for a while they say, "Okay, we need to discuss our relationship. I need to know where you see this going. Are you serious about the relationship? What do you see happening with us? I need to know; I've wasted my time before." They issue ultimatums.

What these women need to understand is that commitment is very easy to see. The way you know someone is committed is that they're there—just as the way you know someone is rejecting you is that they're not. Anyone who has been divorced should understand that someone saying she or he is committed doesn't mean she or he is. You can't establish commitment just by saying you are committed.

In their insecurity and desire to pin things down, women take men who are committed and tell them they're not committed, and that they have to become committed. They invalidate the man's commitment and invalidate it—until they're right. They destroy their relationships by trying to tie them down.

Many of these commitment killers are women in their thirties or forties who feel their time is running out, particularly if they want to have children. They try to pin a relationship down because they are afraid it won't unfold properly on its own. They are afraid that it will disappear, so they try to hold on to it.

If you are in this situation, I empathize with you. But attempting to put this in a box will only backfire. You have to lighten up. You have to realize that in your hurry to establish a commitment, you are killing the natural commitment that is already there.

This is something women need to know how to deal with. And if they're dating men over thirty, they *really* have to know how to deal with this.

First, you need to help your man identify what he is feeling. Second, you have to have compassion for what he is going through. This is a big risk for him, and it can be very frightening. Third, you shouldn't take it personally. This is not about you. It's not about hurting you or about whether he loves you. This is about him. If you want to get hurt, go hit your head against the wall, but stay out of this process. He's not going to stick around if he thinks he's hurting you.

When a man comes up against his fear of failure, your job should be to help him get over this hump. Fighting it, feeling bad or upset, taking it personally, condemning him or trying to force him to stop feeling that way will only make it harder for him to get past this stage. You have to encourage him to risk it. You have to give him assurance rather than feeling hurt and invalidating yourself. You have to deal with this from a position of strength.

You should respond with confidence to a man's fear of taking a risk. Instead of "Don't you love me anymore?" or "When are you going to be sure of our relationship?" or "Why don't you send flowers anymore?" you should say, "I know you're not sure everything is a hundred percent perfect and failure proof, but we have something great and you're going to have to risk it. The water is warm; come on in."

This problem isn't an easy one to deal with, but if you don't, you could end up destroying a good relationship. The same men you've pronounced unavailable end up getting married to women who know how to help them get past their fear of failure.

If a relationship is good, it will unfold in its own time and its own way. Given room to breathe, it will flourish and expand naturally. But when you try to direct how and when it develops, you interfere with the natural flow of things, which is never a good idea. If you're having a good time and this relationship is making your life better, stop trying to get it somewhere.

What about the risk that if you don't force the issue, you'll waste your time with someone who doesn't end up committing to you?

Unfortunately, there's no way around this dilemma. The only way to find out whether a relationship will last is to get deeply involved in it, all the way to the point that it either works out or it doesn't.

As long as a relationship is unfolding and progressing, you should stick with it and enjoy the process. Your relationships are not just valuable as stepping-stones to Mr. or Ms. Right. They are worthwhile simply because being involved with people enriches your life. Letting go of your concern over "where it is going" will enable you to live your life more fully right now.

Instead of regarding a relationship that doesn't end in commitment as a waste, take the point of view that each person with whom you get involved is helping to prepare you for your lifetime mate. I learned something from every relationship I had before I met Tony, and I don't consider any of them a waste.

Having said that, it is also important to realize that there are some men who simply will never commit and with whom you will never have the kind of future you want. Staying in a relationship that is going nowhere will only keep you from being available for one that can give you what you want. Again, the best way to gauge whether yours is a dead-end relationship or one with a future is to go by the physical evidence. I would place my bet on someone who is there all the time while protesting that he's not ready to commit, rather than on someone who pledges undying love but is always working or traveling or unavailable for one reason or another.

marriage

For many people, commitment is synonymous with marriage. I advise people not to get married until they already are. If the love and commitment are not there, getting married won't get them there. If they are there, you're already married. Then you have a ceremony as a celebration of that. I personally believe in marriage, because I think "going public" in this way creates a kind of community support. Relationships are tough; you need all the support you can get.

Left to their own devices, many men would not express their commitment by getting married. Therefore, it is often up to the women to provide the impetus for taking this step.

A lot of women have told me, "If he loved me he would want to marry me." Not necessarily. Marriage is not a man's sport. There is no such thing as "Groom Magazine." You don't hear men saying, "My whole life I've had the dream of standing there and watching my wife come down the aisle. I've always looked forward to renting a tuxedo and choosing a silver pattern."

After I had been living with Tony for about eighteen months, I knew it was time for us to get married. I already knew that we loved each other and that we were both committed to this relationship. I said, "Tony, I think it's time for us to get married." He said, "I don't really want to." I said, "Fine. I was thinking June or September." He said, "Okay, make it September." In the end, because we wanted to have our wedding on a boat on Puget Sound, we got married in July.

This approach worked because it was not about Tony proving that he loved me or that he was committed. I knew he would never volunteer for marriage, but I also knew that this was not a reflection of how he felt about me. It was the generic male resistance to marriage. To pull this off, you must be absolutely certain of the relationship.

My inspiration for this approach was my friend Claire. She was a real master—and it's a good thing she was, because her boyfriend, Martin, had the most severe allergy to marriage of any man I've ever met.

Claire and Martin had been living together for seven years when she told him it was time to get married. He didn't want to. But he didn't want to lose her, so he agreed.

They asked me to meet with them to help them plan their wedding. When I arrived at their apartment at the agreed-upon time, Martin wasn't home yet. Normally a punctual person, he arrived forty-five minutes late.

The three of us sat down with our lists and pages of notes and started to plan the wedding. Martin got up to get something from the kitchen and came back ten minutes later. We resumed the meeting. Five minutes later he left abruptly to make a phone call. This sort of thing went on for about an hour.

Finally, I asked Martin what was wrong. "Nothing," he said. Claire said, "You don't want to get married, right?"

There was a pause, then Martin sighed and said, "No, I don't."

I thought Claire would cry or get mad or be devastated, but she just said, "I understand. What do you want to do about this?"

Martin said he wanted to go out for a walk. After he left, I turned to Claire and asked, "Are you devastated? Does this mean the wedding's off?" She said, "No, it just means he doesn't want to get married. He never wants to go out and run either, but he does it anyway, and then he's always glad afterward. This is the same kind of thing."

"Don't you feel bad that he's not enthusiastic about marrying you?" I asked. "Of course," she said. "I would like it better if he were sweeping me off my feet instead of kicking and screaming over this, but I know he loves me and that he's committed to this relationship. When he talks about not wanting to do it, I don't argue with him. I just keep going forward with our plans because I know this is a process he needs to go through."

As it turned out, Martin got over his resistance later, not sooner. He had second thoughts until his wedding day. But the wedding proceeded as planned, and they have been happily married for the past twenty years.

In working with hundreds of men, I have met very few who wanted to get married. I have met lots, however, who got married.

step 10 assignment

Think about past relationships that ended because of a conflict over commitment. Imagine another way you could have responded. What can you learn from the mistakes you've made in this area?

Afterword
how not to fail

if you've ever run a marathon, you're probably familiar with the phenomenon known as "hitting the wall." It usually happens somewhere between mile 15 and mile 20. Your body feels as if it's going to collapse. You're exhausted, dispirited, in pain, nauseous. You desperately want to give up. But runners who keep going after they've hit the wall often find they get the burst of energy and renewal of stamina they need to finish the race.

You may experience a similar phenomenon after the first few months of following the steps in this book. In fact, the going is likely to get pretty tough, and even rugged souls may be tempted to bail—especially when, after you finally meet the woman of your dreams and have spent five blissful (for you) weeks, she decides to go back to her ex.

Or after your best friend sets you up with a guy who sounds perfect—a surgeon who has a wonderful ski cabin and is going scuba diving in the Galapagos next spring. And then you meet him. He's got acne and halitosis, can't make eye contact, and is not a surgeon but an orderly.

It's then that you start having thoughts like:

"I must not really want a relationship."

"I have great friendships; I don't need to be tied down."

"Maybe some people aren't supposed to have a relationship."

"It will happen when it's supposed to. Trying too hard is what is causing me to fail."

"I need to work more on myself."

"I'm too old (fat, short, poor, tall, skinny) for this kind of relationship."

"It's not worth it."

"I'll do it later when I have more time, energy; when my kids grow up."

Thoughts like these make you want to give up. Don't. Giving up is the only thing that can prevent you from finding a relationship.

It is not the prettiest, thinnest, handsomest, richest, or most famous people who find relationships. It's the people who do something. The more you do and the quicker you do it, the sooner you'll have a relationship. If you give up and stop going for it, there is a chance you'll meet someone. But this may be the most important relationship in your life. Do you really want to leave it to chance?

This is your life—now, today. This isn't a practice life. Don't live it as if it's only a dress rehearsal for your next life—in which you'll do everything right. You're not going to get another chance.

You can have a relationship. I know this. I've seen this approach work for all kinds of single people for more than twelve years. You can have not just any relationship, not even the relationship of your dreams, but one that is better than your dreams.

The only way you can fail is if you give up.

So, don't give up.

appendix of step assignments

*

1. List all the reasons you have used to justify why you don't have a relationship: for example, I'm too discriminating; there aren't enough single men/ women in this city; no one wants someone with kids. It should become evident that many of these excuses just cover up your fear that being single means there is something wrong with you.

2. List all the reasons why you are ashamed or embarrassed about the fact that you don't have a relationship: for example, it means I'm unlovable; it means I'm too needy.

3. List all the reasons why you are ashamed or embarrassed about the fact that you want a relationship: for example, it means I'm desperate; it means I can't make it on my own.

Take a minute to honestly evaluate whether the concerns you listed in exercises 2 and 3 are legitimate or just bogus ideas you have unwittingly accepted.

4. Write an essay entitled, "Why I Want a Relationship."

5. Tell five friends you're looking for a relationship.

stop wishing and hoping assignments

1. Choose a support person/partner.

The first thing to do once you make a commitment to finding a relationship is to enlist the aid of a "partner" or "support person," someone who is also committed to seeing you reach your goal. It can be a man or a woman, a single friend, a married friend, or a relative. The ideal partner is another person who is also looking for a relationship.

Being able to talk to this person when you feel discouraged and knowing that she or he is there to support you will make your project a lot easier and help ensure its success. Now you can say, "I went to a party and talked to five men/women," and not have to hear, "How could you do that? I'd never do that." Instead, a good support partner might say, "How did you do that? I want to be able to do that, too."

Your support person must be someone who is willing to get tough with you if that's what's needed. If you say, "I'm too busy to go out," she or he should say, "I don't want to hear any excuses—do you want a relationship or not?"

2. Make a promise to your support person about a specific action you will take this week that will help you move toward finding a relationship.

3. Write an essay about your "ideal relationship."

List the qualities that are important to you: how you are together, what you do together, how you communicate. Don't describe what you want in terms of what you don't want. For example, instead of, "He doesn't place a lot of demands on my time," say, "He is respectful of my life and my commitments." Instead of, "She doesn't try to change me," say, "She makes me feel appreciated and adored."

Share the essay with your partner.

set yourself free assignment

If you are in a dead-end relationship, break it off. If you think you'll be in danger of caving in, use your support person.

be a great catch assignments

1. Smile and say hello to fifty people a week.

The way to approach this is to make it a game and really go for it. Don't say, "I work at home; I don't see that many people in a week." The idea here is that to reach your quota of fifty smiles and hellos within one week, you're going to have to go to places where you will see members of the opposite sex.

Those places exist in everyday life. You will find you can spot people to smile at while standing in line at the bank or the post office, on an elevator, buying a latte or a newspaper, or at the dry cleaner or car wash.

Margaret, who took my course in Seattle last year, woke up on Sunday morning realizing she had forty smiles left to do before the "deadline" on the next night. She positioned herself at the finish line of the Seattle marathon and smiled at the runners as they finished the race. (Besides being an efficient way to complete the assignment, it helped alleviate Margaret's concerns about safety. She figured someone who had just run 26.2 miles would not be likely to hassle her).

To her delight, both men and women came up to her to thank her for being there, and to tell her how much her smiles had encouraged and supported them. She not only went over her quota of fifty smiles, she is presently married to one of those runners.

So don't be surprised if some outrageous things start to happen.

Even though I'm married, I still smile at people. It's how I meet interesting people all over the world.

Participants in my seminars often complain that people don't return their smiles or make eye contact. Not everyone will—and that's okay. The point of this exercise is not for you to *get* fifty smiles but to *give* them. Why do you think I set the number at fifty? That way, even if the majority don't respond, you'll still probably end up meeting one or two people. And if you do, this exercise will have been a success.

Occasionally, women will express concerns about the dangers involved in smiling at men. Some places are better than others for meeting members of the opposite sex.

2. List ten qualities that make you a great catch. Ask yourself, "What special and unique attributes do I bring to a relationship?" If you can't come up with a complete list, ask your friends to help you.

3. Assess your appearance and wardrobe. Get help from your support person or from someone who has good taste and whom you can trust to be honest with you. Use the Appearance Checklist to evaluate which aspects of your appearance are working for you and which aren't.

Appearance Checklist

	ACTION (*if needed*)	*	BY WHEN
Hair			
Skin			
Teeth			
Weight			
Exercise			
Clothing			
for work			
for play			
for dating			
accessories (shoes, belts, jewelry)			

	ACTION (*if needed*)	✳	BY WHEN
Eyewear (glasses, contacts)			
FOR WOMEN: makeup nails			
FOR MEN: facial hair			

4. Purge your closet.

Wearing clothes in which you do not feel attractive diminishes your self-esteem. If you're like most people, you're happy with only about half the clothes in your closet. The remaining items are "things that might come back into style," "bargains," and the forty-three old shirts you're keeping to wear next time you paint.

Each time you bought a pair of pants, a sweater, or a skirt on sale, you probably said, "For $30 I can't go wrong." But guess what. You've gone wrong twenty times for $30.

It's time to clear out everything in your closet that does not help you look and feel your best.

If you're like most people, you're going to need help on this one. Remember: You're the one who got yourself into this mess in the first place. Pick someone who will be ruthless in forcing you to get rid of anything that doesn't make you look your best.

5. Complete the following sentences:
   I am waiting until I'm married or in a relationship to:
   Have (e.g., a home, insurance, investments):
   Do (e.g., travel, learn to ski):
   Feel (e.g., successful, adventurous):

get out there assignments

1. Continue to smile and say hello to fifty people a week.

2. Conduct a personal interview.

   Use the "ice-breaking questions" on page 71 as a guideline. You can do this with someone you're dating or, if this is too frightening, with a friend.

3. Research dating services in your area.

   Find out how they operate: Do they use videos, personal interviews, or actual matchmaking? Consider which approaches would be most comfortable for you. Inquire about the different programs they offer and compare costs. Check out some of their tapes or profiles. Ask for references.

4. Research local on-line services.

   Using the above guidelines, explore options for connecting with people in your area via modem. Inquire about free trials.

5. Respond to a personal ad.

   Read ads in different local publications until you find one that appeals to you. Answer one or more ads.

6. Write and place a personal ad.

   Using ads you like as a reference, write your own ad and place it in a local publication. If you don't get many

responses, don't take it personally. Take it as an indication that your ad was ineffective and write another one.

7. Join a club, sign up for a class, or get involved in a
new activity in which there is a likelihood of meeting
members of the opposite sex.

8. Ask five friends to support you by fixing you up and
remembering to think of you for parties and other activities. Tell them you just want to start going out and
meeting some new people, that they don't have to be
responsible for finding the perfect match for you. Most
important, if they do fix you up, don't criticize their
choice. Don't say, "What were you thinking," or
"Thanks a lot for the creep you set me up with." If you
do, don't expect them to ever fix you up again.

9. Make a promise to your support person about a specific action you will take this week to advance your search
for a relationship.

10. Get a date.
      Women: Tell a man you're interested in him and
would like him to ask you out. Do this with as many men
as necessary until one of them takes the bait.
      Men: Ask as many women out as necessary until one
of them accepts.

places to meet people

attend sporting events:

* golf tournaments
* tennis matches
* basketball, baseball, or football games

participate in athletic activities:

* softball
* volleyball
* aerobics or health club
* triathlon training club
* sailing or windsurfing
* jogging club
* horseback riding
* bicycling club
* hiking or mountaineering club
* swimming or scuba diving
* river rafting
* dance classes (ballroom, country western, salsa, etc.)

take a course:

* boating
* art appreciation
* fly-fishing
* investments
* carpentry
* painting
* photography
* cooking
* needlepoint
* weaving
* language lessons

shop in:

* grocery stores, especially on "Singles' Night" (if available)
* men's/women's stores

* bookstores
* sporting goods stores
* computer stores
* cosmetic counters
* wine shops
* camera shops
* hardware stores
* car dealerships

attend cultural events:

* gallery openings
* plays (including the discussion groups)
* museums

volunteer:

* in a hospital
* to help a political candidate
* at a public television station
* as a tour guide
* in an art museum
* to participate in a fund-raising event
* to collect for a charity
* for a tournament sport

hang out at:

* racetracks
* marinas
* auctions
* libraries

* coffeehouses
* museums
* AA meetings
* car washes

and:

* travel alone or go on a singles' trip
* go to bars during "Happy Hour"
* join or start a singles' dinner group
* eat breakfast out alone near business places
* visit the zoo (many single parents are there with kids)
* take a ferry ride
* take your niece or nephew to the park
* teach a class or workshop
* go to trade shows
* join a choir or singing group
* go to singles' events
* attend religious services
* go to political events or party meetings
* connect through local on-line singles' bulletin boards
* connect in line (at movies, grocery stores, banks, etc.)

for men: ten good places to meet women:

1. Get involved in the arts

2. Cooking classes

3. Arts and crafts classes

4. Fashion shows

5. Horse shows

6. Aerobics classes

7. Yoga classes

8. Cosmetic counters

9. Dance classes

10. Garden clubs and tours

✱ *for women: ten good places to meet men:*

1. Golf courses or driving ranges

2. Computer stores

3. Hardware stores

4. Car auctions or rallies

5. Auto supply stores

6. Sporting events

7. Fly-fishing classes

8. Boat shows

9. Skeet-shooting classes

10. Political events

just say yes assignments

1. Describe the kind of person you have thought of as "your type." Include physical characteristics, profession, and personality traits.

2. Have a conversation this week with three men/women who are not your type.

3. Get in touch with someone from your past who was interested in you but who you "screened out."

4. Write your "no" list—the criteria you have used to screen people out. Write down every reason you have given for not going out with people in the past: for example, he's bald; she's too short; she has red hair; he doesn't make enough money. Now, pare your list down to only three items that represent core values.

get used to rejection assignments

1. Validate your progress.

Schedule a meeting (or a phone call) with your support person to review the progress you've made so far toward finding a relationship. Talk about what this project has been like for you, what you've learned, what insights have been most important, and what you are most excited about. Be sure to let your partner know how her or his support has made a difference.

Don't dwell on your fears and doubts, although it's okay to mention them. The purpose of this assignment is to validate your successes.

Don't tell your partner, "It was great that I overcame my fear and told that guy I found him attractive, but since he never asked me out, I guess it didn't make any difference . . ." Acknowledge even small signs of progress: that you found yourself smiling at people spontaneously; that you told your neighbor you're looking for a relationship; that you went out with a woman who you didn't think was "your type." Every step you take is getting you closer to your goal.

adjust your attitude assignments

1. Answer the following questions:
   * What problems or complaints have you had in your past relationships? What hasn't worked?
   * What has worked in your past or present relationships? (Think about your most satisfying relationships and list the qualities that were present.)
   * What do you think you would have to give up if you were married or in a relationship? (For example: freedom; closet space; control over your time or money.)
   * The trouble with men/women is: (For example: men are babies; women are after one thing; men are after one thing; men are insensitive; women are too sensitive.)

2. Interview two happily married couples about their relationships: Ask about how they met, their first impressions of each other, the ingredients that make their relationships successful, and whether either had a fear of commitment and, if so, how they resolved it.

3. Relationship collage: You'll need poster board, glue, scissors, and a pile of magazines. Go through the magazines and cut out images and words that illustrate what you want in a relationship (you may want to refer back to the "ideal relationship" essay you wrote in the step 2 chapter). Make a collage out of these images and any other items—photographs, drawings, meaningful objects—you would like to include.

People sometimes say they think this exercise sounds silly. It's not. It helps you get in touch with your vision of what a relationship can be and makes your ideal seem less vague and more tangible and attainable. Many of the same people who resisted doing this exercise reported afterward that they found it moving and inspiring.

No two collages ever look the same. Just use your imagination and creativity—and have fun.

When you're finished, show your collage to your support person and explain to her or him what the images represent to you. You may want to hang it somewhere in your home as a source of inspiration.

don't blow it assignment

Think about past relationships that ended because of a conflict over commitment. Imagine another way you could have responded. What can you learn from the mistakes you've made in this area?

about the author

nita Tucker is a recognized relationship expert who has appeared on *Oprah!, Sally Jessy Raphael, Sonya Live,* and many other broadcast and print media. Nita has successfully led many seminars on dating and relationships to sold-out audiences in more than twenty cities across the United States. Nita's dynamic seminars have inspired thousands and given people effective tools and techniques for finding a relationship—the very same tools and techniques found in this book. Nita Tucker lives in Santa Fe, New Mexico.